LEARNING PARTNERSHIPS

How Leading American Companies Implement Organizational Learning

Robert P. Mai

Maritz Performance Improvement

With contributions by Jerry McAdams

ASTD

AMERICAN SOCIETY FOR TRAINING AND DEVELOPMENT	1640 KING STREET BOX 1443 ALEXANDRIA, VIRGINIA 22313-2043

IRWIN
Professional Publishing®
Chicago • London • Singapore

Irwin Professional Book Team
Senior sponsoring editor: *Cynthia A. Zigmund*
Marketing manager: *Kelly Sheridan*
Project editor: *Susan Trentacosti*
Production supervisor: *Lara Feinberg*
Assistant manager, desktop services: *Jon Christopher*
Manager, direct marketing: *Rebecca S. Gordon*
Designer: *Larry J. Cope*
Cover designer: *Tim Kaage*
Compositor: *ElectraGraphics, Inc.*
Typeface: *11/13 Palatino*
Printer: *Quebecor*

Times Mirror
Higher Education Group

Library of Congress Cataloging-in-Publication Data

Mai, Robert P.
 Learning partnerships: How leading American companies implement organizational learning / Robert P. Mai in collaboration with Jerry McAdams.
  p. cm.
 Includes bibliographical references and index.
 ISBN 0-7863-0388-3
 1. Employees—Training of—United States. 2. Communication in organizations—United States. 3. Learning. 4. Organizational effectiveness—United States. I. McAdams, Jerry. II. Title.
 HF5549.5.T7M229 1996
 658.3′12404—dc20   95–21265

Printed in the United States of America
 2 3 4 5 6 7 8 9 0 Q 2 1 0 9 8 7 6

Dedicated with gratitude to my parents

The only thing that we can really make is our work. And deliberate work of the mind, imagination and hand . . . in the long run remakes the world.

Edmund Wilson

Preface

- Do you work in a "learning organization"?
- Does organizational learning occur in ways that keep you customer-focused and competitive?
- In your company, is organizational learning mainly a responsibility for managers?

This book gives you an easy way to answer the first question (in Chapter 1) and helps you address the second. It also presents an alternative—and, we will argue, a more effective—approach to the issue raised in the third question. That approach we call *bottom-up learning*.

This book brings to its readers a way to get practical about organizational learning. It offers new ways of framing key issues in organizational change and renewal. It approaches organizational learning not as a mandate for "personal transformation" or more management seminars, but as an opportunity for all-employee activity that can put teeth into *empowerment* and results on the table. The **learning partnerships** that we have seen taking shape in leading American companies describe, in fact, a more full-scale, whole organization approach to learning and change.

This book is about real examples of organizational learning, drawn from more than 200 American companies. It relates actual strategies, successfully applied, across a range of industries: automotive, transportation, telecommunications, healthcare, financial services, metals, entertainment, publishing, food service, wood products, and utilities. And it describes organizational learning initiatives in terms of results, as well as of process and methods.

The State of the Learning Organization

"Learning is an idea in good currency," says Harvard professor Chris Argyris.[1] Argyris and other, largely university-based experts have brought to the surface of our business consciousness the idea that organizational learning is *the* key strategy for staying competitive. The new champions of the *learning organization* argue that in order to flourish in changing markets and technologies, companies must learn how to reinvent their organizations through systematic learning.

Like all new ideas that capture the attention of the business world, the concept of the learning organization can probably be said to share these characteristics:

- It's timely, provocative, and somewhat ambiguous.
- It holds great promise and seems to subsume other agendas and issues.
- It is widely mentioned, but unevenly understood.
- It burns brightly for a period of time, then gives way to the next exciting idea.

Most of what has been written about the learning organization so far, according to another Harvard professor, David Garvin, "remains murky, confused, and difficult to penetrate." Moreover, it tends to focus on "high philosophy and grand themes, sweeping metaphors rather than the gritty details of practice."[2] Although an engaging concept, the learning organization has by now caused its share of frustration and exasperation among many who have tried to pin it down and to make it work.

The Practice of Organizational Learning

While the idea of the learning organization will have its window of notoriety in the business press, the concept of "organizational learning" has a much longer pedigree, and is ultimately more useful for practitioners. We'll offer a working definition of organizational learning early on in Chapter 1.

Some years ago, there was a wonderful, full-page advertisement in a Chicago newspaper that captured the spirit of organizational learning as we'll present it. The ad was dominated by a photograph of what was clearly a factory worker: a grimy, middle-aged woman wearing a somewhat disheveled workshirt, gripping a wrench, with a no-nonsense look on her face as she stared out at the reader. The single line under the photo read, "Management Consultant."

Much has been written about how to tap this source of consultancy. We have borrowed strange-sounding words from the Japanese. We have invented an alphabet soup of acronyms with "Q" as the common stock. And we have invoked terms like "continuous improvement" and "systems thinking" to set major renewal efforts in motion.

Progress has been made. But we're still not always sure about how things fit together: how one initiative connects with another, and how they all reinforce continuous and measurable improvement. In this book, we'll argue that *organizational learning is the platform on which we can build many performance improvement initiatives.* As a concept, it's the basis for understanding organizational change and renewal. And as a process, it provides the continuity for a variety of organizational endeavors that aim to sustain competitive advantage.

Making the Case

This book developed around a growing awareness, from our experience working with client companies, that most commentators on the learning organization had too narrow a focus. What we were seeing among the various approaches and strategies that seemed most effective in supporting organizational learning was a pattern of *broad employee involvement.* In some cases, this involvement was attached to a department, or a function. In other cases, close to 100 percent of all the employees in an organization participated, voluntarily.

Learning activity that was so inclusive, and which sustained itself from the energy that only large numbers of people can bring, is an important contribution to the conversation about learning organizations. The practice of learning from the bottom up and from the outside in, rather than the more traditional scenario where *managers* see a light first, then pass it on down, is, we think, the exciting reality of organizational learning today. That's what *Learning Partnerships* is about.

We've organized the book into three sections. Each one has its own introduction, so all we'll say here is that Part II is the stuff of practice sandwiched between slices of conceptual material (Part I) and alternative strategies and implications (Part III). All of the examples concerning practical approaches to organizational learning are drawn from actual client accounts with the Maritz Performance Improvement Company.

Putting this book together was a learning experience in itself. We realize that its usefulness to you, the reader, will turn on a related, but different, kind of learning experience. In both cases, we are individuals attempting to build knowledge and understanding of benefit to organizations. The learning for both author and reader moves us back and forth between stories about companies and uses to be derived from those stories. And the outcomes for both of us, we hope, will be such as can help our organizations work smarter and more effectively.

Robert Mai

Acknowledgments

Writing this book involved a gathering up of many stories—accounts of business experiences from a wide variety of organizations. Some of the stories were told through interviews, and I must first thank those individuals who generously granted me their time to respond to my extended questioning: Bob Stolz at American Airlines; Mark LaNeve, Kurt McNeil, Jeff Pritchard, and Greg Warner at Cadillac; Red Maynard and Alton Russell at Ford. All of these individuals were helpful too in checking my copy for accuracy, and I am grateful for that assistance as well. Lois Stilwell at American Express Financial Advisors, Jay Batz at Ameritech, Diane Gilch at AT&T, Pat Mercurio at Boatmen's Bank, Burl Osborne at the *Dallas Morning News*, Jerry Howie at Ford, Ellen Kidd at Fort Sanders Health Systems, Ben Alexander at GS Technologies, and Marty Raymond at Saturn also receive my thanks for checking up on my "stories," and making them better.

All of the accounts that comprise the meat of this book are stories about clients of two companies: Maritz Performance Improvement and Maritz Marketing Research. I received several different kinds of help from my Maritz colleagues. Some helped me understand their clients better, put me in touch with other knowledgeable people, and offered suggestions about content. They include Gary Allen, Rick Austin, Neil Boyle, Joanne Cuddeback, Pam Donoghue, Mike Ecker, John Foley, Greg Goodman, Al Griffin, Malcolm Haney, Doug Hartman, Janis Heaney, Rose Hull, Kimberley Kritlow, Michael Kuppe, Tom Lawrence, Marsha Littell, Brian McMaster, Mark Nesslein, Nancy Patcha, Michelle Slater, Greg Smith, John Stafford and Janet Viselli. Without their help I could not have written the book, and I thank them. I'll also thank those others whom I've inadvertently left off this list, and ask their forgiveness.

I'm particularly grateful to John Boul and Ron Duchek of Maritz for digging into their information files and sharing their well-researched and crisply written copy. They are true collaborators in this effort. Thanks go too to Jim Winnerman for helping the collaboration happen.

I got special assistance from Yolanda Adams and Gina Wild-Breadon in coordinating the rather complicated affair of building a book from so many different sources. Yolanda Adams was also an invaluable production coordinator and keyboarding consultant. My thanks to them for helping me get the job done.

My friend Peter Wilson at the Danforth Foundation helped me with a thoughtful critique of my early chapters. Thanks also to my colleague George Cesaretti for reviewing these same chapters, giving me good, usable feedback, and adding some deft computer graphics. Sid Hutchins gave the entire manuscript a careful reading, and I especially appreciate his many "catches."

To undertake a project of this size and scope, involving so many of our clients, I needed the sponsorship of my management. I got that from Mark Tucker and Steve Maritz, and I appreciate their support. Thanks as well to Carol Wofsey for her ongoing counsel.

This book was hatched from a presentation that my friend and colleague, Jerry McAdams, and I made at *Training Magazine*'s annual conference. Since then, Jerry has been my main collaborator on this book. His critique of work in progress was continuously sound and insightful, and he contributed many suggestions to strengthen the argument and the flow. He also showed admirable patience with me, since some of his good advice took awhile to sink in and take hold. I'm especially grateful for all his help.

Robert Mai

Contents

I

A CONTEXT FOR ORGANIZATIONAL LEARNING

The major part of this book is given over to examining how lead-ing American companies foster organizational learning, especially "bottom-up learning." But we'll begin by establishing some context. In the first chapter, we'll address the idea of the *learning organization* from the standpoint of how it facilitates strategy development for performance improvement. We'll propose an alternative word choice for framing any discussion about learning as a force for organizational improvement and renewal. And we'll ground this alternative in some research and thinking about learning in organizations. Finally, we'll examine the rela-tionship between individual and organizational learning, and the challenge to capture individual knowledge for organizational purposes.

In Chapter 2, we'll review how learning takes place in organiza-tions. We'll look at a widely accepted distinction between two types of organizational learning, and take issue with it. We'll go on to visit some current ideas about effective learning strategies, like *action learning* (which we find quite relevant), and *adult learn-*

ing theory (which we consider specious). And, we'll establish a focus that will take us in a rather different direction from much of the contemporary thinking on the learning organization.

Chapters 3 and 4 will then review some of the leading *barriers* to organizational learning. Our consideration of learning barriers, both here and in Part II, starts from the following three premises:

1. To understand how to get things done is to understand what prevents them from getting done.
2. There are basic patterns of resistance to organizational learning that can be identified, and anticipated.
3. The key to being practical, and successful, with organizational learning is to plan how to counteract these resistances, or barriers.

These two chapters on barriers to organizational learning establish a critical foundation for our later discussion about building successful learning initiatives. Chapter 3 will concentrate on what we call *barriers of perspective,* or vision problems. We'll look at how people in organizations regularly impose blinders and other constraints to learning on themselves. We'll also address the phenomenon of organizational silos as an impediment to learning. Chapter 4 follows with a discussion of *barriers of motive.* It examines how fear, the need for control, and the problem of success can inhibit organizational learning. These barriers to learning will then provide the logic for the discussion in Part II on how companies cause organizational learning to occur.

Part I is the more theoretical section of this book. We'll be tapping into the research and thinking of a variety of management and organizational development scholars. Our purpose here is to establish a solid grounding for our understanding of organizational learning, and how to make it happen.

We think that such a grounding will pay dividends in handling the practicalities of designing organizational learning efforts. However, readers who want to get practical quickly may choose to go directly to Chapters 3 and 4. There you can visit our treatment of learning barriers, and then move on to the discussion of real-world examples of organizational learning practices in Part II.

Chapter One

Shifting Our Focus

The singular "learning organization" should be a pluralistic model.

Nevis, DiBella, and Gould[1]

By now, the idea of a learning organization has an established place in the language of business, and more particularly, in the literature of business improvement. The term itself is compelling. It seems to be right for the times. In what has been called the *age of information*, the logical response of companies that want to get ahead is to become something called a learning organization.

Already there is a sizeable body of advice on how to become one: a growing literature of business self-help books and articles that vary in scope and sophistication. With so many business thinkers lining up to give shape—and spin—to this concept, the definition of the learning organization is predictably somewhat sprawling, and somewhat elusive.

We'll not try to invent still another one for this book. Instead, we'll be borrowing from a range of people like Chris Argyris and Donald Schön, who really got the ball rolling, and Peter Senge, who made it a bigger ball.

CHASING OUR TAILS

As we see it, the problem with **any** definition of the term *learning organization* is that it teases us with the notion that we might be able to look over a business organization, perform some systematic assessment, and then reach a conclusion as to whether it fits the definition. "Yes, that's one over there. That company is definitely a learning organization."

So far, we don't have an accepted set of standards to size up learning organizations as we have the Baldrige Award as a paradigm for quality. No doubt there are roadmaps and metrics in the works, just as there are already books with titles like *Seven Steps to a Learning Organization*. The problem is that the lack of codified standards typically doesn't prevent us from acting as if some in fact existed.

Therefore, it is also possible to fall prey to a sort of definitional fallacy, wherein we can get caught up wondering whether our company meets some implied set of specifications: Are we really a learning organization, or do we fall short? And if we're not one now, how can we become one?

Inevitably, the learning organization, or any such honorific term, becomes a badge of status that companies find themselves coveting. The business press goes through the exercise of singling out some select companies to be duly recognized, and the rest of us add them to our list of benchmarking targets.

At its worst, the idea of a learning organization can be rather misleading, inviting attempts to emulate models—or be judged against standards—that don't exist. As we have seen in recent decades, this kind of activity can amount to so much game playing, where the players concern themselves mostly with wearing the attributes of the model like the latest fashion. Corporate PR is kept busy, 10-best lists are created, and invidious comparisons are made.

A MORE PRAGMATIC APPROACH

To avoid this tendency to infer a model when none exists, we will be guided by two simple premises regarding the concept of the learning organization. These premises will also serve as the platform from which a book like this one can be written and provide what we hope will be useful and usable information.

First, we'd like to steer around the trap that the learning organization is actually a place, and one that sits on the top of a hill. So we offer the following premise, which places no organizations on hilltops, but instead regards all organizations residing in an open field.

FIRST PREMISE
Every organization is a learning organization

Learning doesn't happen in some organizations and not in others. To designate any one company as a learning organization and by implication to relegate others to the status of nonlearning is simply wrong-headed and disfunctional. What does seem to happen is that learning may happen more quickly, or more thoroughly, with more lasting effect, in some organizations than in others. But all organizations engage in it, even the ones that seem unable to change in the face of new technology, or adapt to new market conditions, or succeed against new competition.

By starting off with this premise, we allow ourselves the opportunity to engage with the idea—really more of a metaphor—of the learning organization in a friendlier, and more serviceable, way. By agreeing that the metaphor should not denote some imagined exclusivity, we may approach it more as a way to describe certain kinds of activities that all organizations engage in, and which are necessary for success.

This argument then brings us to our second premise.

SECOND PREMISE
Some organizations learn better and faster than others

This statement seems both obvious on its face, and also rather liberating. It allows us to focus on a truly productive set of questions, which have definite action implications:

- What are the goals of organizational learning?
- Who participates in organizational learning?
- What are the barriers to learning in organizations?
- How do organizations overcome these barriers?
- How do organizations support continuous learning?

These are in fact the questions that will focus us throughout the book. It seems that to explore the activity of organizational learning is indeed a more fruitful enterprise than to probe the identity of something called a learning organization. In this chapter, therefore, we'll develop a working definition of *organizational learning*, and examine some underlying assumptions and understandings.

WHAT IS ORGANIZATIONAL LEARNING?

Let's start simply. For our purposes, organizational learning means gaining knowledge that helps the organization perform successfully. Now, let's elaborate a bit. Knowledge is gained in at least two ways. The first way is by *acquiring* it, as from a market research study, or by observing another company's operations. The second is by *creating* it, as in figuring out the solution to a problem, or recognizing that another company's operating approach might yield advantages for our own company.

The first way is usually more deliberate and planned: Knowledge is clearly sought after. The second way, creating knowledge, can be deliberate too, as in an experiment. But it is often a byproduct of some other activity, sometimes the result of serendipity. Much of the organizational learning activity we will describe in this book will fall into this second category. But the more mundane means of gaining knowledge—by acquiring rather than creating—can't be ignored. It's less dramatic, but it also produces results.

Ulrich, Von Glinow and Jick point out another critical dimension of organizational learning.

Organizational learning involves "the ability to *generate and generalize ideas with impact*." [2]

This dimension connects the gaining of knowledge to its impact on the organization's performance. It is typically referred to as knowledge transfer or dissemination. Our definition needs to acknowledge the importance of generalizing ideas, and to imply that without the efficient transfer of knowledge, we may be able to claim more knowledgeable individuals, but little or no *organizational* learning. The point will be explored further in the section that compares individual and organizational learning.

The sense that knowledge needs to be productive—to have an impact on performance—is also an important gloss on our definition. Organizational learning is a matter of acquiring, creating, and then disseminating knowledge that yields new and different behavior. Knowledge can lead to new behavior because it either enables behavior to happen, or it prompts behavior to happen, or both. If behavior isn't new, then, by our definition, learning hasn't occurred.

INDIVIDUAL AND ORGANIZATIONAL LEARNING

Using the word learning to describe an activity of organizations may sound like a bit of a stretch when you think about it. It implies, for one thing, that we can regard an organization as if it were an individual—as a biological and psychological entity, if you will. Let's head off this dilemma quickly by agreeing that organizational learning too is a bit of a metaphor. So while organizational learning may be allowed to carry some scientific freight, we won't hold it strictly accountable to the rules of learning psychology (such as we know them).

Rather, we need to work up some further definition for organizational learning in terms of its relationship to individual learning, and in particular, how one can be the consequence of the other. As Argyris and Schön remind us,

> There is no organizational learning without individual learning, and
> . . . individual learning is a necessary but insufficient condition of organizational learning.[3]

That is to say, for organizational learning to take place, individual learning must occur, and something else must occur as well. In our first pass at defining organizational learning, we called attention to the aspect of *transfer* of learning within the organization.

But transfer and dissemination involve more that just the mechanics of spreading around some new ideas.

In Chapters 3 and 4, we'll examine some of the barriers to knowledge transfer. For now, though, we'll merely call out a fact noted by most observers of organizational learning: If an individual has some knowledge that can advance the organization, it is still necessary to persuade others—to help them unlearn as well as learn—so that this knowledge can become institutionalized. As Arie de Geus has remarked,

> The level of thinking that goes on in the management teams of most companies is considerably below the individual managers' capacities. In institutional learning situations, the learning level of the team is often the lowest common denominator.[4]

Capturing Individual Knowledge

Two other ideas about the relationship between individual and organizational learning might be mentioned here as well. The first derives from an obvious, but easily overlooked, aspect of individual knowledge: Much of what we know, especially regarding craft knowledge, is not articulated. It is tacit. It is knowledge that an individual can well demonstrate, but cannot necessarily put into words—at least not readily.

Yet equally obvious is the importance of sharing any piece of knowledge that can improve operating practice, or add value to other parts of the enterprise. So a fundamental requirement for organizational learning is to help individuals make explicit, and transferable, that which may be only implicit in how they understand and do their work.

In later chapters we'll show how a new kind of companywide suggestion program can help bring this tacit knowledge to the surface, and then effectively apply it. Time after time, these programs—when designed with the right incentives and the right support—produce incredible yields *during the first few weeks*. Such quick yields had to have come from ideas that already existed in some form, held by individuals who for whatever reason neither sought to articulate them or to share them.

The conclusion we draw from this experience is that in many companies there is a literal wealth of knowledge that individuals are walking around with, but which has failed to register as organizational knowledge. It has simply never been captured by the organization. In many cases, it has never been articulated in such a way that it could be captured.

Who Are the Agents of Organizational Learning?

The second idea has to do with whom we consider to be the individual contributors to organizational learning. The following explanation by Argyris and Schön of how individual learning becomes organizational learning will help us develop this idea.

> We can think of organizational learning as a process mediated by the collaborative inquiry of individual members. . . . Their work as learning agents is unfinished until the results of their inquiry—their discoveries, inventions, and evaluations—are recorded in the media of organizational memory, the images and maps which encode organizational "theory-in-use." [emphasis added] [5]

The term *theory-in-use* is a critical piece of Argyris and Schön's picture of organizational learning. It refers to the set of knowledge, understandings, and opinions that inform our actions. Lately, the term *mental models* has come into vogue. It means essentially the same thing. Theory-in-use is the stuff of organizational learning.

To change and advance organizational theory-in-use is to improve organizational performance. Within our metaphor of organizational learning, it is of course individuals who are the real agents of learning. Individuals form and reform their theories-in-use under the influence of the culture and the business practices of their companies. They act collectively, and politically, to transfer their knowledge into organizational policies and practices. In this way, organizational learning happens.

In Argyris's concept of organizational learning, *all* individuals can contribute to the institution's knowledge base. While few would argue against this proposition, much of the literature on the learning organization tends to focus almost exclusively on management's relationship to organizational learning. Implicit in this discussion of manager's mental models (de Geus, Senge, et al.) is that organizational learning is mainly the province of management.

This bias towards managers is partly a consequence of a distinction between two levels of learning that we'll examine later. The position we'll take throughout this book is that organizational learning in fact takes place in real companies at all levels, and that the nature of the knowledge created by nonmanagers is significant in financial as well as strategic terms.

One last point about the relationship between individual and organizational learning. Our definition of organizational learning insists that learning must have some manifestation in the organization's performance. It will also be useful to apply a similar understanding when we talk about individual learning.

Just as individual theories of action may be inferred from individual behavior, so organizational theories of action may be inferred from patterns of organizational action.[6]

Chapter Two

Learning in Organizations

The movement toward learning systems is, of necessity, a groping and inductive process for which there is no adequate theoretical basis.

Donald Schön[1]

TWO LEVELS OF LEARNING

Of all the discussions of organizational learning (and, most certainly, of learning organizations), the most frequently heard is the one about the distinction between two kinds, or levels, of learning. Here's a list of the pairings we've come across, along with their coiners.[2] We're sure there are more out there. The point is that each pairing has been coined to make basically the same distinction.

Single-Loop	v.	Double-Loop	(Argyris, Schön)
Adaptive	v.	Generative	(Senge)
Operational	v.	Conceptual	(Kim)
Superficial	v.	Substantial	(Ulrich et al.)

Our intention in this section is not to draw out the nuances that distinguish one pairing from another. Rather, we'll proceed on the basis that the distinction is useful, but the variations are not. In fairness to the writers named above, there are differences. But in fairness to Argyris and Schön, not much new has been added by a second generation of scholars to improve our understanding of single- and double-loop learning. So we'll stick with the originators.

Single-Loop Learning

In a series of books written in the 70s, Argyris and Schön elaborated a theory that apparently has had wide impact, although that impact took a while to register. The theory stated that we could look at individual and organizational learning as working at two different levels. The first level is called *single-loop learning* to denote what we colloquially call "staying inside the box."

> [C]orporations . . . continually respond to the changing pattern of external competition, regulation and demand, and to the changing internal environment of workers' attitudes and aspirations. These responses take the form of error detection and error correction. Single-loop learning is sufficient where error correction can proceed by changing organizational strategies and assumptions within a constant framework of norms for performance.[3]

Single-loop learning is, to be sure, about more than finding things that don't work and fixing them. It extends to all kinds of initiatives to make things better than they presently are: work procedures, purchasing practices, scheduling, etc. But single-loop learning tends to focus more on knowing *how* to get things done, rather than on *why* we're doing these things, and whether we should instead be doing something completely different. Enter double-loop learning.

Double-Loop Learning

Double-loop learning can be said to involve "outside the box" thinking. It allows that there is often another path to follow in knowledge building that takes us beyond the first path, or loop. Double-loop learning seeks to resolve inconsistencies in our understandings. It probes the basic assumptions and norms that underpin and explain our present theories of action. It asks *why* questions.

> We will give the name "double-loop learning" to those sorts of organizational inquiry which resolve incompatible organizational norms by setting new priorities and weightings of norms, or by restructuring the norms themselves together with associated strategies and assumptions.[4]

Adjusting to new situations can lead to restructuring of fundamental understandings, from which new, more versatile and serviceable understandings emerge. Thomas Kuhn was alluding to this phenomenon when he coined the term *paradigm shift* in 1962.[5] Kuhn's discussion of revolutions in scientific thinking presented a rather grand model of double-loop learning, which we have since watered down somewhat with our incessant use of the term.

Today, all of the exhortations in the learning organization literature telling us to confront and examine our existing mental models, to engage in generative thinking, and to seek breakthroughs, emanate from this notion of double-loop learning. We think the distinction between two kinds of learning is a useful one, but it also can be misleading. For there is, as we noted before in another context, a tendency in the literature to focus much more attention on double-loop organizational learning. Double-loop learning has more spin.

As a consequence, we also tend to underestimate both the importance of single-loop learning, as well as its connectedness to how we come to restructure our guiding assumptions and understandings. Argyris and Schön recognized the artificiality of this distinction, stating that we might speak of organizational learning "as *more or less* double-loop." The workings of single- and double-loop learning suggest to them ultimately a "continuous concept of depth of learning."

> It is possible, we think, to make clear distinctions between relatively deep and relatively peripheral examples of organizational learning. We will continue to call the former double- and the latter, single-loop learning. . . . The reader should keep in mind, however, that we speak of these categories as discrete *when they are actually parts of a continuum.* [emphasis added][6]

In our experience with both manufacturing and service companies, we have seen the power of single-loop learning—especially with problem solving teams looking for ways to improve productivity and quality—to ignite some dramatic rethinking of basic operating premises. We have also seen simple ideas trigger a broader questioning of business policies and practices.

The reverse, of course, is also true. Rethinking fundamental business positions, in turn, demands new organizational learning to be able to operate from these new positions. The massive efforts to reposition companies in deregulated industries, for instance, involve organizational learning of both kinds, and almost simultaneously. The cases and stories that make up the major part of this book will provide illustrations of a range of learning.

AN INCOMPLETE PICTURE

It is our contention that much of what is written about the learning organization presents an incomplete picture of the reality of organizational learning. By concentrating on the learning challenges of managers, and upper-level management more often than not, this literature gives the impression that organizational learning is mainly the province of those normally tasked with more reflective, "big-picture" thinking.

This stance has its roots in the scientific management theories of Frederick W. Taylor, which are almost a century old. For Taylor, planning and thinking about work processes and job design were reserved for a professional, and managerial, class. Workers performed their tasks unthinkingly; otherwise, they might disturb the well-engineered work routines laid out for them. This rigidly hierarchical division of labor also signified a division of learning. Workers were simply not required to contribute to organizational learning.

Today, as progressive an observer of the labor scene as Robert Reich paints an equally dismal picture. In his discussion of emerging occupational patterns, Reich identifies three broad categories of work, but only two sets of knowledge requirements. Workers, Reich argues, will perform either routine production services, in-person services, or symbolic-analytic services. The first two work categories differ only in certain superficial respects. Workers providing in-person services—restaurant servers, sales clerks, secretaries—come into direct contact with their customers. Workers providing production services do not. Both categories involve simple, repetitive job tasks, and are guided by standard procedures and rules. Knowledge requirements are basic skills in either case.

Contrast these characteristics to the attributes of the symbolic analysts. They are the degreed professionals, and their work is to "solve, identify and broker problems by manipulating symbols.

They simplify reality into abstract images that can be rearranged, juggled, experimented with, communicated to other specialists, and then, eventually, transformed back into reality." And, their value to their companies is contingent upon their being able to "innovate by building on their cumulative experience. . . ."[7] In other words, they seem to be the key agents of organizational learning for their companies and their industries.

COUNTERPOINT

No doubt there are many intellectually dead-end jobs around, with no expectation or opportunity for on-the-job thinking, let alone knowledge building. But the neat divisions of work and learning responsibility that Reich describes just don't hold up. They don't hold up against the experience at Ford, or American Airlines, or Cadillac, where nonmanagerial workers are reshaping—and rethinking—the way business is done.

Nor do they hold up against the experiences of countless workforces that are being challenged by information technology's relentless advances which redefine their roles around higher order thinking. Consider the implications of this statement by an equipment operator in a pulp and paper mill about working under newly automated conditions (quoted from Shoshana Zuboff's wonderful *In the Age of the Smart Machine*).

> Before computers, we didn't have to think as much, just react. You just knew what to do because it was physically there. Now, the most important thing to learn is to think before you do something, to think about what you are planning to do. You have to know which variables are the most critical and therefore what to be most cautious about, what to spend time about before you take action.[8]

As Zuboff explains, "the vital element here is that these workers feel a stark difference in the forms of knowledge they must now use."[9] The presence of computerized controls requires of today's production workers an unprecedented opportunity to exercise inferential reasoning, manipulate symbolic information, and, yes, practice systems thinking. Or, as another mill operator put it,

> Things occur to me now that never would have occurred to me before. With all of this information in front of me, I begin to think about how

to do the job better. And, being freed from all that manual activity, you really have time to look at things, to think about them, and to anticipate.[10]

An organization's leadership is, to be sure, the critical force in determining the climate for experimentation and inquiry, as well as for self-examination and the challenging of status quo thinking. But leadership only shares the responsibility for organizational learning. The rest of the responsibility belongs to the rest of the workforce, and we have found that the workforce can be more than equal to the task.

THE JOY OF LEARNING (FOR ADULTS ONLY?)

The good news about organizational learning is that it comes so naturally. The bad news is that it can also involve conflict and bad feelings. This is the good news section. We'll deal with the other in later chapters on barriers to learning.

When we inquire about the nature of learning in the workplace, we frequently come across references to *adult learning theory,* or, if we're not careful, we stumble upon something called *andragogy.* In both cases, an educator named Malcolm Knowles seems to have staked out the territory fairly well and has set forth some widely accepted assumptions about adults as learners.

To most psychologists, and to our perception as well, adult learning theory isn't really theory. It's more a set of commonplace observations bundled together. And andragogy, defined as the opposite of pedagogy (i.e., the teaching of children), isn't what it claims to be either. Adults and children basically learn in the same ways, using the same strategies and having the same motivation. That which Knowles describes as the *learning* tendencies of children are actually the *teaching* tendencies (unfortunately) of most schools.

Here are Knowles's main observations about adult learning:

- Learners are self-directed.
- Learning draws from life (and presumably work) experience.
- Readiness to learn is self-determined.
- There is a strong problem-solving orientation to learning.[11]

As learners in the workplace, we are indeed characterized by qualities like these. We are also characterized by a fundamental orientation towards increasing our competence. This "motive for competence," described by psychologist Robert White in 1959,[12] holds forth great promise for organizational learning. We are, it seems, a species of problem solvers, both as children and as adults. In the right circumstances, which we'll address in subsequent chapters, we take to developing new competencies like ducks to water.

LEARNING HOW TO LEARN

Learning how to learn is one of those catchy phrases we hear fairly often in conjunction with learning organizations. What does it mean? In most discussions, the phrase attaches to the argument regarding the surface-your-mental-models drill. By recognizing inconsistencies in our understandings, we clear the way for significant learning—we're learning how to learn.

We don't want to make any more of this phrase than is warranted. We will, however, reintroduce Robert Reich into the discussion here because we think his description of the skills of the symbolic analyst are in fact the basic skills needed for anyone who is to contribute to organizational learning. Reich names four skill sets:[13]

- **Abstraction:** the capacity to use equations, formulae, analogies, models, constructs, categories and metaphors in order to create possibilities for reinterpreting, and then rearranging, experience; discovering patterns and meanings; bringing order.

- **System thinking:** the ability to see the whole and how the parts are connected; to discern larger causes, consequences, and relationships; to see how one problem may be linked to others.

- **Experimental inquiry:** the ability to learn by systematically exploring a range of possibilities and outcome and drawing logical conclusions; using guesswork and intuition, then testing against previous assumptions.

- **Collaboration:** the capacity to seek and accept criticism from peers, solicit help, and give credit to others; to empathize; to negotiate and work toward win-win solutions.

In later chapters, when we discuss how teams work together to generate useable knowledge for their companies, we'll see these basic skills being deployed.

ACTION LEARNING

Because we're becoming more aware of both the importance of learning in the workplace, and how it can occur there, there's been a renewed interest in the tactic of action learning. Action learning is another of those new packages for sturdy old goods. Its antecedents go back to the turn of the century and John Dewey's progressive education reforms.

Simply put, *action learning* is an approach to learning through on-the-job problem solving, usually in small groups or teams. The critical ingredient in action learning is reflection. Without it, action learning is just action: solving a problem without affecting our capability for acting differently—more competently—the next time a related problem comes up.

The challenge in making action learning happen is to be able to *prompt reflection*—to create reason and opportunity to step back and think about the implications of a problem solving experience, and to extract or create some useable knowledge from it. Action learning is often held up as the antidote to that other learning strategy, training, which typically occurs apart from actual work activity and whose greatest failing is a lack of learning transferred to the job.

Action learning is based on the premise that when action and reflection dance together, either partner can take the lead. Henry Mintzberg, a shrewd observer of behavior in organizations, makes this point well in a discussion of strategy development as an informal, unplanned activity.

> We think in order to act, to be sure, but we also act in order to think. We try things, and those experiments that work converge gradually into viable patterns that become strategies. This is the very essence of strategy making as a learning process.[14]

While some learning organization proponents see problem solving activity, particularly that engaged in by nonmanagerial work teams, as being a relatively inconsequential contributor to organizational learning (because it doesn't redefine the problem, it just seeks to fix it), we do not. What we see is a dynamic interplay between the thinking about how to improve on existing situations and the thinking that occasionally takes us outside of or around those situations into new fields of understanding. One kind of thinking leads into, and sometimes gives rise to, the other.

Given this inevitable connectedness between problem solving and the periodic need to restate, or reframe, the problem, we regard action learning opportunities—for managers and nonmanagers alike—as having much promise for stimulating organizational learning. In the corporate experiences we'll describe in subsequent chapters, action learning has proven itself a powerful engine for change and renewal.

We'll talk indirectly about action learning later on when we examine the ways in which some companies have created exciting opportunities for teams to generate innovative ideas. Action learning typically focuses on real work problems or challenges. There's another strategy that is much discussed in the context of the learning organization, one that simulates problems so as to enhance their learning potential. With this strategy, problems can be future extensions of present realities (called *scenarios* by Pierre Wack when he developed them at Shell), or they may be purely hypothetical—like Senge's "microworlds."

In either case, the intention is to push the learning envelope—to force some introspection and to nudge thinking into new dimensions. Here is Pierre Wack talking about scenario building at Shell.

> We had first tried to produce scenarios that we would not be ashamed of when we subsequently compared them with reality. After our initiation with these first sets of scenarios, we changed our goal. We now wanted to design scenarios so that managers would question their own model of reality and change it when necessary, so as to come up with strategic insights beyond their minds' previous reach.[15]

MYTHS AND MODELS

What does happen when managers, or nonmanagers, for that matter, question their present model of reality? Admittedly, this is where some learning organization theorists start getting goose bumps because it is precisely at this juncture that breakthroughs supposedly occur. The scene that gets sketched in the literature has us surfacing our mental models, discovering them to be inadequate or constraining or both, and then pushing beyond them to a higher understanding of reality.

This portrayal of the events of organizational learning can be useful, in the sense that building models to describe certain logical patterns of action—process models, as we like to call them—is a useful teaching tactic. But models are only abstractions. They're helpful for communicating simplified versions of a messier reality that can't always be clearly or intelligibly observed.

Learning itself is a messy phenomenon. It tends to occur less in the form of the "Aha!" experiences that we might expect to be the consequences of concerted efforts to reframe, think outside the box, etc. For the most part, we probably can't stage such experiences, learning laboratories and microworlds notwithstanding. Much organizational learning is plodding and incremental. At other times it is accidental. But organizations do create knowledge, they do develop significant new understandings, and they do manage to "manage change." Our aim is to document how real business organizations work to do all of this by nurturing and supporting the activity of learning—for everyone.

Chapter Three

Barriers to Organizational Learning
Barriers of Perspective

We have met the enemy, and they is us.

Walt Kelly

Walt Kelly's "Pogo" was on target when it comes to the enemies of organizational learning. As we explore how companies practice organizational learning, it will be necessary first to acknowledge, and then to describe, some of the barriers to learning created by individuals and by organizations. Peter Senge addressed this issue in *The Fifth Discipline* in a chapter called "Does Your Organization Have a Learning Disability?" We'll expand on that discussion, or rather, we'll try to reframe it.

We see organizational learning being thwarted by barriers both unintended and intended. These barriers are sometimes created by the organization, and sometimes by ourselves. They all serve to slow learning down. In some cases, they succeed in blocking learning from occurring at all.

We've chosen to address these barriers, which we've encountered mostly in large corporations, in two categories: *barriers of perspective* and *barriers of motive*. In each category, there are both individual and organizational forces at work that retard learning and change.

We'll admit upfront that any attempt to create a framework of categories can be somewhat arbitrary. Categories have a way of falling into one another if you look at them long enough, and these are no exception. Even with our basic distinction between barriers of perception and motive, we're aware that these two inhibiting forces often occur together, and that either one can be the cause of the other.

Notwithstanding, we'll use this distinction, and the subcategories that follow from it, as a means to get closer to how barriers to learning actually function. To fully appreciate the corporate initiatives we'll describe in subsequent chapters, we must see them, at least in part, as strategies that address specific barriers to organizational learning.

Barriers of Perspective as "Vision Problems"

Much of what doesn't get done in the way of organizational learning is due to what we can't see. That is to say, our perspective of what goes on within our own companies and industries is often severely limited by a variety of barriers. As individual employees, our perspective can be narrowed by task or departmental barriers. We'll call any failure to see beyond the boundaries of task or administrative unit **tunnel vision.** Chris Argyris contends that our perspective can also suffer from self-imposed **blind spots.** Blind spots can be described as "skilled incompetence" that prevents us from noticing inherent contradictions in our actions. Another limitation on our perspective as learners can be attributed to the habit of wearing **rose-colored glasses.** Managers, in particular, seem prone to this tendency. A fourth vision problem, **myopia,** is more a corporate tendency to concentrate on the here and now and neglect the future.

TUNNEL VISION

This barrier exists almost everywhere in complex organizations. It is most commonly seen as the limitation placed on one's perspective by departmental and divisional boundaries. We often refer to this barrier by talking about *silos* or *chimneys*—separate operating or functional units within a business that remain functionally ignorant of one another's needs and ways of doing things.

The tendency to mind one's own business to the detriment of intracompany coordination and collaboration can be explained in part as simply human nature, thus inspiring the following rule:

THE RULE OF TUNNEL VISION

Nobody in a large organization really knows or cares what anybody else is doing.

But silos are also natural consequences of the isolation brought about by bureaucratic structures. Such isolation can be reinforced by deliberate actions to retard information sharing and cooperation. In instances like these, silos tend to place parochial interests ahead of the interests of the larger organization.

Silos inhibit learning. They prevent the inflow of information from outside one's own work area—information that has the potential to stimulate new thinking about the work process and the business. Silos also mitigate against entertaining any sort of broader perspective that might open up new possibilities for learning. One of the most obvious learning casualties of the silo effect is the failure of many productivity improvement efforts to adequately address the interconnects in work processes. Yet it is precisely there, in the places between departmental boundaries—where the hand-offs get made—that the biggest potential for productivity improvements typically lies.

Some of the reasons why silos exist and perpetuate themselves are competitive and territorial in nature. We'll address those in the next chapter, "Barriers of Motive." But others can be explained simply as consequences of force of habit and of natural reluctance to look beyond administrative boundaries. In these cases, tunnel vision can often be effectively countered with the kind of high-energy initiative we'll discuss in the chapter called "A Jump-Start for Learning."

Limits to Learning

By implication, tunnel vision impairs our ability to see the bigger picture. This impairment is not simply the consequence of our inability to see across administrative boundaries. As Senge notes, "There is a fundamental mis-match between the nature of reality in complex systems and our predominant ways of thinking about that reality." Senge is referring specifically here to our tendency to want to view cause and effect as being "closely related in time and space."[1]

This aspect of tunnel vision is perhaps most commonly encountered when we try to solve a work process problem, but confine our solution to our own work area. There are usually two possible consequences if the problem actually involved more than just this specific area. We might discover, in one case, that if the cause of the problem lies at least partially outside our area, our solution won't work. In the other case, we might solve the problem locally, but create three more problems elsewhere in the organization.

The opposite of the condition of tunnel vision approximates what Senge and others refer to as *systems thinking*—understanding things in context, perceiving interdependency within complexity. But tunnel vision not only limits our ability to see the forest for the trees. It also hinders our ability to see the trees clearly and to rethink the parts of a process because we can't derive new insights about the whole to which they contribute.

Indeed, the need for a systems perspective exists to some degree at practically every level in the organization. Increasingly, we need to see how and why things come together. We need to exercise a perspective of synthesis. The growth of access to information, brought about through computer technology and communications networking, demands it. So does the phenomenon of corporate delayering that compels people to operate with information in ways they did not have to in the past.

BLIND SPOTS

Tunnel vision is characterized by lack of awareness of the breadth and depth of an organization and how it works. It is brought about mainly by the administrative boundaries within organizations. Blind spots, on the other hand, are a vision problem we tend to bring upon ourselves. This vision problem is most apparent in cases where we have difficulty seeing beyond a specific task or job routine. It also occurs when we choose to understand job-related issues only according to certain prescribed theories or rules which we feel are professionally, or socially, acceptable.

Blind spots can regularly prevent us from looking beyond our own work, noticing other sides of the business, and seeing how things connect. They can also impair our ability to imagine different ways to get things done. If we've been trained in the methods of a particular craft or discipline, for example, we can easily lock into these methods and be blind to the relative advantages of alternatives. While this problem is encountered most typically within certain professional disciplines, it can operate on many other stages as well. Drucker provides an illustration in a discussion of corporate research:

> The greatest straightjacket for a company today is to be successful in research, because the company believes that the important technological changes are within its industry. In almost all industries today the basic technological changes are outside of it [sic]. So your research lab either has never heard of the important developments or worse, they say, "Well, that's not what we were taught in school."[2]

Blind spots are also incurred by managers when they assume, by virtue of their rank and position, that they have a monopoly on knowledge and the ability to solve problems. Looking back at a successful companywide employee suggestion program, a senior manager of a large Midwestern bank illustrated this blind spot with the following admission:

> Perhaps the mistake I made going in to it was that I underestimated the impact it would have on the organization. Not that we underestimated our people, but when you're in management, you of course think you have all the answers, or certainly have thought about most of them.

Blind spots are often exemplified by a reluctance to seek insight from others on the grounds that, as a professional, or a manager (or even as a company), you simply don't need anyone else's advice.

Hiding Contradictions

Blind spots can also be self-inflicted because people mount clever defenses to hide apparent contradictions. We become adept at ignoring discrepant experiences or at rationalizing discrepant events. As Argyris puts it, our "counterproductive actions are actually highly skillful."[3]

An example might involve a case where a supervisor has performed a task her team could have performed for itself. The supervisor explains her action as modeling certain behaviors so the team could learn them, when, in reality, the behaviors were more motivated by her desire to get the job done quickly. And besides, she didn't really trust the team to do the job right. The supervisor's explanation is not intended as a lie, but represents instead a skillfully designed rationalization that allows her to have it both ways—in her own mind.

Argyris makes a distinction between what he calls our *espoused theories*, the way we tend to explain our actions to others, and our *theories-in-use*, the real guiding reasons behind any specific set of actions. Much of the time, our espoused theories and our theories-in-use are congruent and consistent. But in some instances, particularly when we are dealing with nonprogrammed, difficult, and threatening situations, they are not. The most important point that Argyris makes concerning this kind of occurrence is that we are often unaware—or only tacitly aware—of the inconsistency.[4]

The blind spots in our understanding of why we do what we do are obviously a potential hindrance to learning. This is especially true with professionals, who are likely to espouse theories that are consistent with their particular professional methodology, although their actions might be guided more by pragmatism and expediency. Professionals also are frequently given to analyzing problems, but are rarely able to see themselves as part of the problem. These observations give rise to "the rule of blind spots."

THE RULE OF BLIND SPOTS

Any problem of understanding is always someone else's problem.

Blind spots can indeed be a consequence of our own intellectual arrogance. One antidote to this vision problem is a dose of humility regarding the value and validity of other perspectives. In many organizations, the flattening of hierarchies is forcing this dose upon the survivors. Another tactic used to treat this problem, much written about in learning organization literature, is to help people bring to the surface and examine the ways in which they currently construe reality. Such an activity might also need to involve an examination of the defenses we employ to maintain our blind spots. We'll touch on such defenses later in this chapter.

ROSE-COLORED GLASSES

Many of us work, or know of people who work, in environments where it seems a lot safer to accentuate the positive and not be the bearer of any kind of organizational bad news. These are good-news organizations, where people collude to restrict the flow of certain kinds of information that may in fact be of great value for organizational learning.

This collusion is especially apparent in what happens to the upward flow of information in an organization. Thus, the "rule of rose-colored glasses":

THE RULE OF ROSE-COLORED GLASSES

The quality of information declines as it moves upward through bureaucracies.

In effect, what we're seeing here is people who reside on the upper rungs of the corporate ladder being fitted for rose-colored glasses by people beneath them. And so long as managers acquiesce to this way of receiving information, the value of that information for organizational learning purposes will be compromised.

This phenomenon of protecting people from hearing bad news

is of course not restricted to upward flowing information. One of the most underused knowledge building opportunities is the systematic debriefing of completed projects or jobs. There are several reasons for this, but one is simply that most companies are reluctant to examine things that might not have gone right. "Mistakes were made" is a line we want neither to hear or to utter. Dorothy Leonard-Barton and her colleagues in the Manufacturing Vision Group cited this failing in their review of development projects:

> Some of the 20 projects that the group studied were audited after their completion, but the review was not systematic. Sometimes the reviewers were reluctant to highlight problems, fearful that doing so would embarrass people and appear unfair.[5]

Since a development project is potentially a fine action learning opportunity, not to take full advantage of the potential for fear of hurting someone's feelings, or even bruising a reputation, is in the end a disservice to valuable organizational learning. When this vision problem becomes chronic, the consequences to the organization can range from debilitating to disastrous. Conversely, an organization that allows for negative feedback or critical comments, delivered without any protective airbrushing, is an organization that's prepared to learn from its experience.

MYOPIA

Most organizations suffer from myopia, or nearsightedness. The major symptom of this barrier of perspective is the tendency for people to be so caught up in the day-to-day rush that they can't see beyond the next deadline. They're always too busy with today to take a longer term perspective on their business. Five-year planning routines notwithstanding, myopia is probably as naturally occurring a vision problem for companies as it is for individuals.

There seem to be two schools of thought on this vision problem. Both need to be considered in order to make a proper diagnosis and before any treatment can be recommended. Proponents of the first school counsel for a continuous quest for foresight and the need to have a well-informed point of view about the future.[6] Without this perspective on the future, their argument goes, we are locked into a restrictive present orientation. Our business strategies will tend to concentrate merely on catching up or staying even with the competition.

In today's turbulent business conditions, such an orientation hardly prepares us to deal with future opportunities, not to mention future dangers. It's rear-guard and stodgy, and most likely dooms the enterprise to premature obsolescence. Following this logic, learning organization proponents like to exhort us to focus learning not so much on *fixing* things as on *reinventing* them, to meet customer expectations of the future!

Well, yes, but only up to a point. As the "rule of myopia" reminds us,

THE RULE OF MYOPIA

Nearsightedness is not corrected by looking through a telescope.

The antidote for myopia is not a prescription for glasses that only see the horizon. Remember that Pierre Wack, the Shell planner who developed future scenarios as a learning exercise for managers, was less concerned about trying to predict the future than he was in helping his managers examine their present frames of reference. We are also aware, with Argyris and Schön, that short-term, adaptive thinking can sometimes lead into transformations of considerable scope and impact. And this brings us to the second school of thought on myopia as a barrier to learning.

Chaos Theory

These days, any discussion of long-range planning, or of learning as a quest for foresight, must be tempered by the inferences that scholars in various disciplines are drawing from the new science of *chaos*. Here is management scholar Ralph Stacey on the subject:

> When a system operates in chaos, it is highly sensitive to small changes. It amplifies tiny fluctuations or disturbances throughout the

system, but in a complex way that leads to completely different, inherently unpredictable forms of behavior. Because tiny changes . . . can so completely alter the behavior of the system, its longterm development depends in effect upon chance.[7]

Chaos theory states, therefore, that the long-term behavior of a complex system, like the marketplace, for example, cannot be predicted with any certainty. Instead, we must come to regard any such system as inherently disorderly and unstable. So, while myopia in organizations is still a problem, the implication for confronting it is not simply that we need to become more farsighted.

Rather, we need to maintain a "constant scan" mode so as to take in as much as possible, being alert for changes large and small in the environment. We also need to develop and extend our feedback systems so that we can observe more acutely that which is actually happening in the present. It would seem, in fact, that what we really need to learn, as individuals and as organizations, is not how to become less nearsighted, but more *clear-sighted*.

RECOGNIZING THE "ENEMY"

Our challenge with barriers of perspective, in general, is first to be aware that they exist. Next, we need to be able to recognize them in their several different forms. Only then can we begin to counter their influence as barriers to organizational learning.

Chapter Four

Barriers to Organizational Learning
Barriers of Motive

The resistance to change exhibited by social systems is much more nearly a form of "dynamic conservatism"—that is to say, a tendency to fight to remain the same.

Donald Schön[1]

The impact that barriers of perspective have on organizational learning is usually inadvertent. With barriers of motive, however, the effects on organizational learning are often deliberately intended. Barriers of motive include all the reasons why people choose (or influence others) not to behave as learners when given the opportunity to question, solve problems, experiment, and examine new ideas. We'll explore two types of motives that work against organizational learning: **fear** and the **need to be in control.**

Since this discussion is about barriers, we'll address motive as a negative force. In subsequent chapters, we'll review how companies attempt to engage positive motivation, including rewards and recognition, to stimulate learning behavior.

FEAR

The motive of fear prompts defensive behaviors. Those behaviors can include resistance to, or avoidance of, activities with learning potential. This is especially the case where risk taking is involved.

Without trying to be inclusive, we'll discuss several different kinds of fear that inhibit learning.

Fear of Failing and of Losing Face

Learning on the job can be risky business. It can expose the employee as a slow learner, wherein he or she is compromised in the eyes of peers and bosses. Or it can be frustrating and anxiety-producing when we're called on to learn new routines or deal with difficult problems, especially for the first time. Avoidance of any learning challenge that threatens either to compromise or frustrate a worker is a commonplace occurrence at any job level.

Avoidance behavior can frequently take the form of what Argyris calls defensive reasoning:

> Defensive reasoning encourages individuals to keep private the premises, inferences, and conclusions that shape their behavior and to avoid testing them in a truly independent, objective fashion.[2]

The steps we take to avoid seeming incompetent, feeling vulnerable, or being embarrassed, are wide and varied. One of the most obvious tactics is to dodge activity that involves confronting the unknown. But the unknown, of course, also contains the potential for developing new understandings. Not feeling confident enough to talk about our perceptions, or to test our assumptions, inevitably serves to short-circuit individual and organizational learning opportunities.

Still another variation of this barrier to learning is the fear of appearing different and nonconforming, and therein threatening one's social acceptance by the work group. Fear of nonacceptance often causes individuals to seek quick consensus in group decision making. When the desire for consensus overrides the possibility of more prolonged investigation or of voicing an opinion contrary to the prevailing one, then the individual is essentially opting for a nonlearning course of action.

The "New Work Relationship"

One of the ironies present in today's workplace derives from this phenomenon of fear and passivity and attaches to the concept of *empowerment.* Empowerment has become the "E" word in many places, and thus attained a rather dubious and unpromising status. But the strategy to assign to employees greater responsibility *and* greater access to resources, including information, is clearly inevitable given the trend toward flattening hierarchical structures. More than ever before, companies are calling for a new relationship between managers and employees. They're asking employees to step up to a new level of challenge.

However, this call to assume more responsibility comes at a time of higher perceived risk. Downsizing and restructuring convey to many employees that the new rug they're being asked to step onto could be yanked away at a moment's notice. Even when a management team is sincere about establishing a "new contract" regarding the sharing of control, communication and reward systems will not automatically change long ingrained habits of passive, dependent behavior.

At its worst, this problem shows up as a handing over to management of *all* responsibility for solving problems. Argyris observed this decidedly non-learning posture in a company where employees had settled into a comfortable and undemanding relationship with their management.

> They claimed to value empowerment when in reality they valued dependence. They claimed commitment to the company when in reality they were commited only to the principle that management should make all the tough decisions.[3]

Here the fear of taking risks, and a reluctance to assume responsibility for risk-taking, undermine the potential for organizational learning on a broad scale.

Fear of Punishment

We touched on this barrier earlier when we looked at the impact that reengineering and downsizing has had on the American workplace. Wherever job security is threatened, fear of job loss tends to render workers at all levels more guarded and conservative and less likely to take risks. When employees have experienced continued downsizing and reorganization, as they have in the deregulated telecommunications industry, for example, this guardedness can become chronic. Yet ironically, it is precisely at this time of renewal that the organization can most benefit from fresh and innovative thinking.

An environment of change and upheaval prompts many companies to try a variety of programs aimed at regrouping and refocusing the remaining work-force. Because each of these programs stays in force about as long as it takes for the next management shakeup, employees have good reason to fall back upon the most basic of defenses. Edgar Schein cites the most common of these defenses against regrouping to be:

1. Not to hear the message in the first place,
2. To deny that the message applies, and
3. To rationalize that our leaders do not understand the situation.[4]

But fear of punishment and loss does not have to wait upon reorganization to happen. A far more common incidence is fear of being punished for a mistake on the job. The following statement, made by a section supervisor in a Ford engineering group several years ago, captures the problem and what's at stake with some eloquence:

> People used to deny and hide mistakes around here, because they were punished. Superiors assumed we were all goof-ups; they wanted to know *whom to blame,* not what went wrong. In fact, though, a mistake signals that there is a flaw in the system. Something that permits a conscientious person to do the wrong thing or to neglect something. *That's* what you want to track down and eliminate. Punishment creates a fear of failure, and that kills creativity.[5]

In a work climate where the response to experimenting and taking risks is likely to be a reprimand, the behavior that is conditioned into the workforce is of course much the opposite. Very little learning occurs other than how to protect yourself.

Quality guru J. Edwards Deming felt so strongly about this that he included the admonition to drive fear out of the workplace as one of his founding principles for performance improvement. And Schein too sees decidedly negative consequences to organizational learning from the efforts made to avoid such punishment:

> Avoidance behavior learned through punishment . . . does not tell the learner what the correct response is and does not encourage trial

and error learning. People who are punished across a wide range of behavior are likely to limit themselves to very narrow safe ranges or become paralyzed for fear of making mistakes.[6]

Over time, fear of being punished for mistakes and errors can create deep resistance to learning in an organization and severely retard that organization's ability to tap its workforce for any kind of new thinking or innovation.

THE NEED FOR CONTROL

The *need for control* is mostly thought of in terms of management behavior. In fact, however, it occurs much more broadly, and it subverts learning in different ways. Argyris has observed from his research in organizations that people generally adopt behavioral strategies aimed at controlling their environment, including other people:

> There seems to be a universal human tendency to design one's actions consistently according to four basic values:
> 1. To remain in unilateral control;
> 2. To maximize "winning" and minimize "losing";
> 3. To suppress negative feelings; and
> 4. To be as "rational" as possible.[7]

It is not our intention, in examining this barrier of motive, to do a psychological study of the controlling personality. Rather, we'll try to set forth some ways in which the need for control can be opposed to organizational learning. Then we'll zero in on a particular aspect of control in organizations: the control of information.

Argyris's conclusions about this universal tendency implied that it pertains to most people in most organizations. The need for control is, in this sense, a condition of the workplace that we need to acknowledge and cope with. Here are some of the oppositions that Argyris's four basic values suggest. For the purposes of our discussion now, we'll merely identify where some conflicts may lie. In a later chapter, we'll return to the business of resolving those conflicts.

1. **To remain in unilateral control** implies a reluctance to delegate to others significant problem solving responsibilities. It would also suggest the unlikelihood of extending much authority to teams or to team members. "Empowerment" would be a rather empty concept. Differences of opinion and conflicting positions would be squelched.

2. **To maximize "winning" and minimize "losing"** would suggest a strong aversion to risk taking and experimentation. It would also tend to support internal competition and silos, as opposed to cooperation and openness.

3. **To suppress negative feelings** would inhibit serious reflection and critical examination of the status quo. Furthermore, it would make problem identification and continuous improvement efforts unlikely.

4. **To be as "rational" as possible** would lead to an avoidance of issues that resist easy explanation, as well as areas that are unfamiliar. Doubt or uncertainty would likely be denied rather than confronted. Experience tends to be interpreted through a rigid cause and effect logic. Getting "outside the box" would be a difficult trip.

There are of course other implications for organizational learning that derive from this cluster of controlling tendencies. Collectively, they serve to retard learning. They are, by definition, not so much defensive behaviors as they are premeditated and even aggressive. They range from attempts at controlling the thinking of others, at one extreme, to unyielding allegiance to certain ideas thought to be responsible for past "winning," at the other.

The Information Tollway

Thought control as a concept smacks more of a practice to be found in totalitarian political regimes. But it exists in corporations in less insidious fashion as the control of information. If information is the food of thought, then there are rich diets and poor diets, depending on the organization's approach to information sharing and the means of information access.

Historically, information flow downwards through a bureaucracy has tended to be highly controlled. Managers have generally regarded information as an element of their power, essential to their ability to exert control over those below them in the hierarchy. What their employees don't know, however, is also a limitation to their ability to think on behalf of their organization and to contribute to organizational learning.

Information access can be severely limited when different offices or departments within the organization regard information as property, to be guarded. We addressed this phenomenon earlier in a discussion of silos. Information is a most controllable commodity, and it becomes a political pawn when silos operate in a highly competitive mode. Unfortunately, organizational learning can be held hostage to these competitions.

In the past few decades, computers and communications networks seem to have conveyed a promise to corporations: that vast quantities of information would be made available to anyone who was connected. But the promise needs to be qualified by the other connotation of "connected." For in addition to having the right network systems, companies also must understand how barriers of motive impact upon information sharing. A study reported on by Davenport, Eccles, and Prusak concluded that these barriers needed to be carefully managed:

> In the most information-oriented companies we studied, people were least likely to share information freely. . . . As people's jobs and roles become defined by the unique information they hold, they may be less likely to share information—viewing it as a source of power and indispensability—rather than more so. When information is the primary unit of organizational currency, we should not expect its owners to give it away.[8]

One of the unfortunate ironies apparent in the age of the information highway is that despite the greater access to information made possible through technology, information doesn't necessarily flow any more freely. Nor does it encourage feedback. What we're now discovering is just how strong the connection between information and the need for control truly is. As it turns out, information in organizations is rarely free in any sense of the word. Instead, it usually comes with costs attached, expressed in currencies of influence and control.

Success as a Barrier to Learning

The greatest obstacles are always the things you did well yesterday, the things you spent 30 years perfecting.[9]

Peter Drucker made this statement, but many have remarked on the problems that success brings to a business. At its base, maintaining the status quo when the business is going well is a natural and logical instinct. We apply colloquialisms like "stick to the knitting" and "don't fix it if it ain't broke" to this essentially conservative posture as if to confirm its undeniable folk wisdom. And there is wisdom here. The trouble is, of course, that while we're trying our best to stand still, the rest of the world is moving on.

These days, standing still is rarely good for business. Unfortunately, it is easier to agree in principle with this statement than it is to abide by its full implications. Most managers in fact would probably support the statement as part of their espoused theories about business. But most of us tend to demonstrate more allegiance, in our theories-in-use, to the tried and true formulas that brought us success in the past. And many managers see their main function being to keep the business enterprise working in strict accordance to formula.

This management function is exercised by monitoring the way adherence to formulas is maintained. It involves process control, but it also involves the reward system that reinforces compliant behavior. Many organizations talk about the value of change and of inaugurating newer, more progressive work processes. But occasionally they find themselves thwarted by an entrenched reward system that reinforces behaviors inimical to desired changes. Sometimes this reward system works directly in conflict with new business directives.

In a study we conducted for a large telecommunications company, most of the components of a broad reward system tended not to be performance contingent. Instead, they merely reinforced basic work responsibilities: working hard, being a good corporate citizen, following management's direction. Rewards would come by virtue of management's good will. The company had, by its own description, an "entitlement culture."

But this company's goals had shifted dramatically. Deregulation forced a strong need to become more competitive and to drive toward specific new performance goals. Yet the existing reward system was basically reinforcing conformance to the old culture.

When a company with an entitlement culture wants to confer more value on competitive behaviors, it must work to overcome a history of acquired—or learned—habits. As Edgar Schein notes,

Our organizational culture, which can be thought of as the accumulation of prior learning based on prior success, typically limits and biases our capacity to perceive and understand a new vision.[10]

Reward systems that are not aligned with the business goals of an organization typically act as a brake to learning. They limit the pace of change.

Stability and the Avoidance of Conflict

The need for control, as a motive force that inhibits organizational learning, contributes to the formation and management of cultural rules and rewards. Cultures, as we've remarked before, want to preserve a stable state of affairs within an organization. If those affairs have led to success, the culture is inevitably strengthened. Behaviors like questioning and critical self-examination, that can lead to significant, double-loop organizational learning, are understandably regarded as disruptive to the prevailing culture. Managers who see their responsibility as preserving a successful enterprise, by controlling against deviation and waywardness, will tend to discourage such behaviors.

A wonderful illustration of how a culture reinforced by success can stifle change comes from a recent account of how another telecommunications company, Ameritech, went about managing change. Like many Bell system companies, Ameritech had developed its business practices over long years of facing virtually no competition. Its habits were ingrained. Employees felt comfortable there:

> Real issues were not discussed, let alone thrashed out, because everyone took great care not to rock the boat. Hardly anybody—at any level—was ever fired for lack of performance. In many instances performance was measured poorly or not at all, and there was no reliable feedback to let employees know how they were doing. People felt entitled to increasing paychecks, great benefits, and rock-solid job security. It was the quintessential "lifetime" company, a natural outgrowth of a monopoly industry accustomed to cost-plus pricing.[11]

As with the development projects studied by Leonard-Barton, the lack of objective feedback, coupled with a reluctance to be critical about fellow employees, contributed very little to employees' ability to learn from their experience. Avoidance of conflict—related to Argyris's finding regarding the suppression of negative feelings—was practiced to a fine art:

> Ameritech managers were polite. . . . They took great care not to hurt one another's feelings, especially in public. They had known one another for a long time because they had all risen through the ranks. . . . It was an insular, well-ordered world, adept at protecting its own and resisting all manner of change.[12]

Avoidance of conflict for the sake of preserving the stability of an organization is a logical strategy to follow. So is treading lightly over problematic issues because they might point to the need for change if pursued too heavily. Ameritech faced up to its challenge. It went on a crash organizational learning course that led to restructuring, downsizing, and a new vision of its business goals and how to pursue them. We'll revisit Ameritech in a later chapter.

Ameritech found, as have many other large companies, that managing change was a complicated task. The most difficult part involved challenging its managers' fundamental attitudes about the requirements for business, and personal, success. Stacey sees the dilemma as one that turns on the issue of organizational stability and instability:

> The actions managers design depend on what they believe about the nature of success. If they believe that instability is an inherent and necessary feature of a successful business, they will seek to provoke certain kinds of instability. If, on the other hand, they believe that instability is the enemy of success and is due simply to incompetence and ignorance, they will seek to banish all forms of instability.[13]

Stability can be controlled for in a variety of ways in corporations. At least two of these ways can have deleterious effects on learning. One is controlling against the evolution of core capabilities or competencies (because they're wrongly perceived as a guarantee to continued success). Another is imposing controls against experimentation and R&D (because of too narrow a financial perspective and an overemphasis on cost control). The former can lead to missed opportunities, especially involving new technologies. The latter, caused by "financial myopia," a barrier of perspective, can curtail valuable development efforts and the learning that attaches to them.

Conflict as Resolution

It is interesting that several organizational learning theorists, including Argyris and Schön, Schein, and Stacey, all seem to agree that some level of conflict is both inevitable and probably required as the antidote to the problem of stagnation.[14] The strategy of this book is to discuss how to counter barriers to learning in the ensuing chapters. But we'll cheat a bit here, partly because conflict can also be regarded as a barrier itself.

Indeed, if conflict leads to stalemate and retrenchment or provokes fear and self-protectiveness, it definitely acts as a barrier to organizational learning. But when adherence to older approaches (that have produced past successes) frustrate people who see a need for change, the resolution to this dilemma might well be some open confrontation. As Argyris and Schön suggested almost 20 years ago, incompatible visions for sustaining competitive advantage "are characteristically expressed through a conflict among members and groups within the organization":

> In the industrial organization, for example, some managers may become partisans of growth through research and of a new image of the business based upon research, while others may become opponents of research through their allegiance to familiar and predictable patterns of corporate operation. Double-loop learning, if it occurs, will consist of the process of inquiry by which these groups of managers confront and resolve their conflict.[15]

We'll return to this issue of conflict that spurs organizational learning when we examine how "constructive conflict" can be staged to good learning advantage. To close this chapter on barriers to organizational learning, and to round off the discussion on past achievement as an inevitable barrier to continued success, we'll refer to a quote by economist Kenneth Boulding:

> I have revised some folk wisdom lately; one of my edited proverbs is "Nothing fails like success," because you do not learn anything from it. The only thing we ever learn from is failure. Success only confirms our superstitions.[16]

II

STRATEGIES FOR ORGANIZATIONAL LEARNING

If these are the barriers to organizational learning, how have companies dealt with them? Part II of this book is about approaches taken by leading companies in manufacturing and service industries to counteract barriers of perspective and motive and to make organizational learning happen. The approaches we'll describe were in most cases strategies to achieve specific business ends: cutting operating costs, generating new revenue, raising customer satisfaction levels. Learning and knowledge building were the means to these ends.

The companies we'll make reference to were typically quite conscious of the means they were deploying. They made plans to engage diverse groups of people: employee groups (and in many cases, that meant *all* employees), trade allies, customers. They created support structures, made useful information accessible, and trained people to take full advantage of it. They provided incentives and other reinforcements to insure that people would see these activities as a priority, for both the company and for themselves.

The activities these companies sponsored were initiatives in performance improvement and self-renewal. They sought measureable business advantages as outcomes. They set goals for themselves, made resources available, and invited broad participation. They understood that in a world of change, trying to create advantages that would play out into the future would require more learning than planning and more process than plans.

They also discovered that the forms organizational learning might take could change over time. What started out as a venture in reengineering might take the shape later of an all-employee suggestion program, and still later evolve into a version of continuous quality improvement. What characterizes all of the examples presented in this section is an aim to involve more than management in the process of organizational learning. Customers are asked for input, as are suppliers, distributors, and other business associates. But most of all, these companies sought to invite their own employees to become partners in the process of organizational learning. How these partnerships took shape, and how they were managed, is the subject matter for the following chapters.

The organizing principle for Part II will be the barriers to learning, and how companies have worked to overcome them. Chapters 5 through 8 will focus on the four barriers of perspective: tunnel vision, blind spots, rose-colored glasses, and myopia. In Chapter 9, we'll look at how companies have tried to combat the two kinds of fear that inhibit learning and risk taking. Chapter 10 addresses the need for control, and how sharing control has become a means to more effective learning at Cadillac. We'll conclude, in Chapters 11 and 12, our review of how companies are neutralizing barriers of motive with lessons from American Airlines and Ford in dealing with the barrier of success.

Chapter Five

Breaking through Boundaries

Innovation is usually found in organizations and societies that create structures, processes, rewards, and status systems that encourage it: that build extensive networks that enrich the possibilities for learning by doing, and that systematically clear obstacles from innovation's evolutionary path.

Anthony Carnevale[1]

In this chapter, we'll visit several companies seeking to improve performance through knowledge building. More specifically, we'll look at examples of efforts where employees were challenged to devise ways to improve existing work processes and existing sources of revenue.

To borrow from Carnevale's prescription above, teams were typically the *structure* these efforts employed. The *process* involved problem solving and innovation. And in each case, the company made deliberate provision for *rewards* and *status systems*, or recognition. Our special focus will be on how these team initiatives sought to cross company boundaries that limited both knowledge building and learning. In other words, how companies attacked the organizational learning barrier of tunnel vision.

```
                        CASE PROFILE
```

EPIC HEALTHCARE GROUP

This story begins when Kenn George, a former senior official in the Reagan administration, brought together a group of 36 hospitals (and five financial service centers) to form EPIC Healthcare. Job 1 was to build an organization that linked this network of independent hospitals, each with its own culture and management. Job 2 was to reduce operating costs while at the same time improve the quality of care.

George had begun by building a central management team, commited to open communication and participatory management. He located the corporation's headquarters in Dallas and called it the "Support Center." He also put into place an employee stock option plan, or ESOP, to underline the corporation's commitment to employee ownership. The new culture of EPIC Healthcare would be one of participation and shared responsibility. But George understood that employee participation and ownership in a healthcare organization was hampered by the rigid administrative divisions that tended to keep key functional groups separate.

Separate might actually be a euphemism here, since hospitals have been described by some observers as comprising not just silos, but armed silos—at least three of them, manned respectively by doctors, nurses, and administrators. George's view was that "Health care is traditionally a hierarchical framework of management. I was trying to create opportunities for interdisciplinary and team participatory management philosophies to pervade the organization."[2]

Thinking as Owners

The strategy that EPIC settled on to energize its more than 10,000 employee-owners in pursuing Job 2 was one that also addressed the silos. EPIC undertook a companywide quality and cost reduction campaign that invited all its employee-owners to *think* as employee-owners—on cross-functional teams. Voluntary teams of seven members each were formed to work together to combine perspectives and know-how. Teams were challenged to submit cost saving or revenue generating ideas. Systems were established to allow teams access to necessary information for idea development. All suggestions were evaluated by committees with expertise in the relevant area.

To promote the crossing of departmental boundaries, team co-ordinators—typically managers or supervisors—were assigned to work with groups of seven to eight teams. The team coordinator could offer technical advice or help connect the team to the right source of information in another department. EPIC also designated key managers, including the CFO, as resource people for teams to go to for specialized information.

As a consequence of these strategies, George was able to observe significant progress towards organizational learning, as well as the neutralizing of silos:

> When you build interdisciplinary teams, when you have to do budgeting as a team because it's against the rules for anyone to do it for you, when you have to do feasibility analyses, when you have to submit what you think an idea will save the hospital or how it will improve quality, when you have to start asking questions of the CFO in the hospital or the pharmacy or whatever . . . [you can] break down the hierarchical inhibitors, the boundaries, that are traditional in this business.[3]

At the end of the first year, EPIC had already established a strong precedent for participatory management throughout the organization. And they had also managed to approve over 2,200 ideas, for a total value of $21 million to the corporation. EPIC's idea generation activity also rewarded team participants. Whenever an idea was approved, the submitting team received credits that could be used for substantial merchandise awards.

The top teams from each of the EPIC facilities also earned a run-through in the warehouse where the award merchandise was stored. Teams were given 60 seconds to grab whatever they could load on a large warehouse trolley. The run-through was both a strategic incentive to sustain activity and to solicit more expansive ideas and a recognition event to commemorate successful knowledge building.

CASE PROFILE

THE *DALLAS MORNING NEWS*

The *Dallas Morning News* is the leading metropolitan newspaper in the Southwest and the only remaining daily in Dallas. Like most companies in the newspaper publishing business, The *Morning News* was facing a downturn in their regional economy in the late 1980s and this resulted in flat advertising revenues and escalating costs. To increase productivity, they had opened a new state-of-the-art production facility a few years earlier. They continued to be interested in extending innovation elsewhere within their business operations.

The management team at the *Morning News* understood that nontechnological innovation would be a challenge. Most newspaper operations are organized along traditional departmental lines and in Dallas one major function, production, was now physically separated from the other areas of the business. Employees tend to maintain their own department boundaries and communications across department lines can often be impeded.

Another important tradition in the newspaper publishing industry is the strict separation of the news and editing staffs from all of the business departments. This serves to protect and preserve the objectivity of the news operations and to insulate them from undue influence or outside interests.

As a result, aside from senior management, few staff entertained a corporate perspective on the health of the business and how to make it better.

Newspaper management decided to address this situation by launching a team-based suggestion initiative. Employees would be invited to develop ideas that could improve operating efficiencies or enhance revenue generation. Team members who submitted approvable ideas would share in the annualized gain their idea brought to the paper.

A Chance to Make a Difference

At the outset, employees did not stampede to form teams. Enrollments were slow. Then teams in marketing and production began to organize. A few cross-functional teams were sighted. And finally, some news staffers and news teams joined in. The program director observed that in the early going teams went after "the low hanging fruit—ideas we'd been carrying around with us. Then, we got creative."

When the dust had settled, newspaper staff were asked to assess the experience and its impact on the paper. One participant from the marketing department observed that "in the end, what interested people in the program was the chance to make a difference, to have their ideas heard, and *acted upon*." This sentiment was echoed by another marketing team member. "The program did create a climate for change here. People will be willing to come forward. I think they believe they'll be heard, and they'll not hesitate to talk to people they were a little wary of before."

While participation levels and idea productivity were high, there were other benefits which underlined the organizational learning strides the company had made. One team leader admitted to a "different way of approaching my job, with a little more open mind, seeing that there are always alternatives to the way we currently do things, and that the way we do it now is not always the best way." Another team leader, a copywriter, noted that for the first time she had had occasion to step back and learn about how the business was actually run. "I was horrified I'd lived in utter ignorance for so long about what goes on in the newspaper. I learned about new technology; I learned about how we deal with customers, how we actually put out the newspaper everyday."

Several members of the newspaper staff addressed the breaching of barriers—and the reduction of tunnel vision. As president and editor Burl Osborne observed, "We managed to tear down walls that had separated various departments. Notably, between the news and production departments."[4] A participant from the classified ads group expanded on this point. "Probably the most important thing I got out of the experience was contacts I made in the circulation and production areas. I've been able to get some things done that I wasn't able to get done before because I know some people in those areas now."

Still another, different testimonial to how a well-designed team-based suggestion activity can attack barriers of perspective came from a member of the program management team. His conclusion was that "many people emerged as leaders. So it gave us a whole different view of people we had kind of put in a slot." The paper's controller summed it up this way: "I don't think this company will ever be the same."

CASE PROFILE

BOATMEN'S BANK

Boatmen's is the largest bank in St. Louis. Like most banking organizations, it was looking for ways to improve competitive advantage through expense control and operations improvement. Boatmen's had conducted an employee survey whose findings posed an interesting challenge for management. Bank employees had essentially said that they thought they knew how to improve the way the bank did business.

Some senior managers were skeptical. The bank had run suggestion programs before, and they yielded only modest results. One manager commented, "We suspected that employees would offer suggestions like 'stop the doughnuts at our meetings.'" But Boatmen's decided to take the survey findings as an invitation to try again, but with a different game plan. This time they would organize around cross-functional teams, provide significant incentive, and make arrangements to quickly capture savings from good ideas.

Here's a firsthand account of their experience, from the perspective of several senior managers:

- We had found in our employee survey that a lot of the different divisions did not know what other divisions did and didn't know people in other areas. We decided to ask employees to work in cross-functional teams, across divisions. We found that not only did they get to meet a lot of people they wouldn't normally have met, but they got a chance to share ideas and find out what's going on in the bank.
- Cross-functional teams allowed people at different levels to interact where they wouldn't have the opportunity to interact in the past. Not only did they learn about their division and how they interact with others, but they got to see the

big picture of how the organization is run and how to get things done in the organization.

- Our people showed that they could come up with ideas that we'd have to pay a high-priced consultant to give us—and in an environment where we've always emphasized expense control.

- We found employees coming up with ideas that would take 20 minutes of programming and offset the bank hundreds of thousands of dollars in cost savings a year. It was the magnitude of ideas that people came up with that we didn't expect.

Boatmen's Bank considered itself to have a highly disciplined expense control culture. They had a practice of taking any significant expense reduction adjustments that developed during the year and incorporating them immediately into their operating budgets. This practice worked to their advantage in reinforcing the seriousness of their team initiative: Any approved ideas would also be quickly worked into somebody's operating budget.

The Boatmen's case illustrates in particular the potential for cross-functional employee teams to produce not just incremental improvements, but complex solutions with sizeable impact. Cross-functional teams are more likely to engage a systems perspective in their deliberations, and to create ideas of grander scope. It is also worth considering that systems thinking at the all-employee level can have a significant effect on silos and the narrow perspective they tend to reinforce.

CASE PROFILE

GEORGIA-PACIFIC

Georgia-Pacific wanted to get a maximum number of employees from all levels involved in suggesting cost reduction ideas. They had another objective too: to open up communications across divisions so as to spread new knowledge and improved operating practices across their more than 80 locations.

Georgia-Pacific mounted a major team-based idea program, involving over 12,000 employees. Many of the ideas that were generated represented modest improvements to existing work practices. Many others were of more extended size and complexity. One plant worker mentioned, "I've had one idea I've been thinking about for 26 years, as long as I've been on the line." He also remarked that several of his colleagues had similar long-considered suggestions to make, and did. "But then," he added, once those ideas were presented through the program, "then, we started *looking*."

Many of the teams that contributed significant new thinking to the business were cross-functional teams. Here are two different ideas, each submitted by a cross-functional team, and each approved and implemented.

- A team in the credit department was concerned over the money credited to customers for products that arrived damaged. While insurance claims covered some of the damage, customers did not receive their material on time. Working with a team member in the shipping department, they were able to come up with an idea that changed the strapping of products on railcars, thus providing a more secure load and dramatically reducing damage en route.

- A team comprised of shopworkers noticed the growing pile of sawdust created during a lumber planning process. Further research indicated the company was paying $25,000 annually for the removal of this waste. The team discovered the sawdust could easily be turned into a mulch that local nurseries would actually pay for. Their idea provided an ecologically beneficial solution to a costly waste problem and brought cost-free revenue to the company.

Georgia-Pacific's second objective was also well met. Davis K. Mortensen, executive vice president, commented that "the communications between the hourly workforce and the salaried, supervisory group improved, I think, dramatically."[5] A wood products division vice president noted that the experience had "drawn us closer to our employees and given us the ability to be more aware of what's going on for them, what they're interested in, and the kind of contribution they can genuinely make to our bottom line." His counterpart in another division added, "I think the biggest thing Georgia-Pacific got out of this was the communication. The financial reward was great, but the lines of communication that were opened will grow forever within Georgia-Pacific."

A plant worker who had participated on a team echoed this assessment of increased empathy and a broadened understanding of the business. "We've always had a relationship, as far as working together, but it seemed like the team program has drawn us closer together. We've been able to understand each other's jobs better, what the other co-worker does in the plant. Plus, the hourly employees are able to understand better what kind of responsibilities upper management has."

A plant supervisor observed that "our employees now know the cost of producing the product. They know how it reflects in their paycheck. They know how it reflects in our overall performance. They know now what it costs to produce a board, and what it costs when we're down, so they know what loss will cost us." All this learning was brought about through the work that teams had to do to present cost estimates for valuing their ideas. All told, more than 4,000 innovations were accepted and implemented: a lot of learning, yielding a lot of knowledge *building*, for Georgia-Pacific.

How Teams Advance Organizational Learning

Each of these cases illustrates the capacity of a companywide team-based activity, focused on knowledge building, to advance organizational learning. Each case also demonstrated that some of the knowledge building occurred because certain administrative barriers to learning and communication were broken through.

There are actually two aspects of team-based idea generation that work to combat the barrier of tunnel vision in bureaucratic organizations. One is the *teamwork* itself: the purposeful blending of different work perspectives to produce new knowledge for the company. Cross-functional teams are the most obvious structure for accomplishing boundary crossing. An article appearing in *Scientific American*, reviewing some recent research on how people learn best in the workplace, provided this confirming finding:

> People learn more swiftly—and so are more effective—when they belong to "overlapping communites of practice," or groups with differing specialties.[6]

The other aspect of team-based idea generation that needs to be recognized here is the *activity required in researching ideas*. When an idea targets more than one step of a work process, and when the interfaces between work functions need to be considered, the team will usually have to extend its knowledge of the process. Other ideas, involving even broader process considerations, can require extensive researching across boundaries.

Even the smallest idea, when it involves doing a cost-benefit analysis, may require the team to obtain some cost information not normally accessed and not a part of the team's normal level of understanding of the business. All of these knowledge developing tasks can call for inquiry beyond the normal purview of the individual work group. In the course of developing an idea, team members learn what kind of information is available, where to find it, and how to use it. Information needs of many an idea team thus lead team members into learning how to learn, both within, and about, their organization.

Criteria for Success

There is already a considerable literature on the subject of effective teams. But our focus here is on team-based innovation and the development of new knowledge that improves performance. Here are seven key elements of the organized team process that contributed to the success of these four companies.

Seven keys for team-based idea generation

1. Promotion as a high-priority, companywide activity fully supported by top management.
2. Encouragement for cross-functional team formation.
3. Significant incentives, tied to the value of approved ideas.
4. Role training for team leaders and evaluators.
5. Commitment to prompt idea evaluation.
6. Commitment to prompt implementation of accepted ideas.
7. Tracking system, covering ideas from submission through implementation.

In the four cases we described above, organizational learning paid both short- and long-term dividends. In the short term, each company realized measureable productivity and revenue enhancement gains. But their experience with team-based idea generation also helped the four companies to appreciate their own potential for knowledge building—and how best to tap that potential. Indeed, their collective experience with a team process, built around the seven key elements described above, yielded them a variety of learning benefits promising future returns.

Learning benefits from team-based idea generation

- Opens communication and learning across administrative and hierarchical boundaries.
- Teaches cost benefit logic and the cost of doing business.
- Extends knowledge about work processes.
- Facilitates big-picture understanding of the business.
- Establishes precedent and opportunity for systems thinking.
- Targets knowledge building as an organizational priority.
- Reinforces individual self-confidence and self-esteem as "knowledge contributors."

Organizational tunnel vision retards knowledge building on a large, companywide scale. It also retards the process of rethinking, or reinventing, the business—a process that is necessary to sustain and extend competitive advantage. Companywide team-based idea generation is a strategy that can overcome the barrier of tunnel vision. It requires playing by certain ground rules, as we reported above. But it is a strategy that pays for itself on several levels.

Chapter Six

Opening Doors

And it is not only interdepartmental barriers which must be demolished; the firm's outer boundaries also need to be radically redefined, so that suppliers, customers, and strategic alliance partners can become insiders and be tapped systematically for ideas and insights.

Matthew Kiernan[1]

In Chapter 3 we remarked on a number of blind spots in organizations that represent barriers to learning. Blind spots are normally the product of various biases and attitudes about the validity of others' points of view. "Not invented here" are frequently the words written on the blindfolds people inadvertently wear.

Thus, engineers might question the understandings of nonengineers; researchers, the knowledge of nonresearchers, and managers, the insights of nonmanagers. Blind spots sometimes extend to whole companies—especially market leaders—or to sectors in a distribution channel, like manufacturers towards distributors. In such cases, people whose reluctance to listen and give credence to the perspectives of others are denying themselves, and their organizations, a valuable opportunity for learning.

One strategy to correct the impaired vision brought about by blind spots is *managing by fact*. Championed by the TQM gurus, managing by fact promotes the use of hard, measurable data—statistical data in particular—to counter the unreliability of opinion and intuition that can undermine business decision making. Another, related, strategy is frequently discussed in the learning organization literature. It aims to establish a routine of questioning assumptions and models of reality, on the grounds that they might have become inadequate, because reality changes and makes old models obsolete.

These two approaches are both viable, and they both speak to the problem. Managing by fact requires training and tools, and a commitment to creating serviceable process control systems. The "assumption questioning" routine has yet to be formalized as an approach. It exists instead as a collection of tactics, described sometimes as planning (see Wack, de Geus, and Mintzberg[2]) and sometimes as learning, or "unlearning," exercises (see Senge et al.[3]). Both approaches tend to involve managers only.

We'll take a different tack in this chapter. The strategies we'll examine on overcoming blind spots are primarily strategies for encouraging *inclusion*. That is to say, we'll look at examples of corporate initiatives to invite other points of view, to create opportunities for joint problem solving, and, in general, to open doors rather than keep them shut. These strategies vary in form and implementation. But they do tend to involve, by definition, many people, in many phases of the making and distributing of products and services. And they've been implemented in real time, with measureable impact on organizational learning.

CASE PROFILE

UNITED ARTISTS

How does a large chain operation identify, and then disseminate, best practices for all its operating units? And how does it continue to improve on the definition of best practices, particularly as market and industry conditions evolve? This was the learning challenge that United Artists set out to tackle.

United Artists employs about 10,000 people, at over 400 theaters in 29 states. For several years they have been engaged in a performance improvement effort that sets standards for theaters in several sales and operations categories. On an annual basis, theater performance is assessed against those best practice standards and rewarded accordingly.

The standards themselves are designed and weighted by task groups made up of a mix of home office staff and theater management. And each year, the groups have a chance to rework, or at least to reweight, the standards in order to align with timely business priorities. The mix and the changing make-up of the task group allows for different, and fresh, perspectives.

But this effort was only tapping the problem solving and creative thinking of the management level. United Artists wanted to involve all employees in a best practice, knowledge-building process, so as to engage still more perspectives and to increase the learning yield. The "bottom-up" approach to organizational learning that United Artists took was designed to work in two phases.

In phase one, United Artists invited all of its theater employees to call in their ideas for improving performance to an 800 number. Ideas could suggest better ways to handle everything from concessions and promotions to film scheduling and training. In just four weeks, almost 9,000 calls were accepted by an independent call center, yielding more than 11,000 ideas.

Before making their calls, employees were asked to write out their ideas in 25 words or less to accommodate easy transcription and sorting by the call center. Employees earned a "crew certificate" worth about $2.50 and an entry in a sweepstakes for their first suggestions. Each additional idea earned employees another sweepstakes entry. Later, after ideas had been reviewed during phase two, additional awards, based on approved idea value, would be made.

In phase two, a United Artists management team sifted through the collected ideas to identify the most promising ones. These ideas were then distributed among some 50 home office teams to document idea value and create an implementation plan. For ideas that were ultimately implemented, these team members could also earn awards based on the fully documented idea value.

United Artists has demonstrated a healthy regard for the power of a workforce not normally thought of as "business consultants" to suggest valuable business improvement ideas. This group of theater managers, ticket takers, concessions clerks, and others contributed more than $3 million worth of performance improvement. They did so because they were asked, because they really were the experts, and because there was an incentive to follow through.

CASE PROFILE

SATURN

Since launching itself as the first new General Motors nameplate in decades, Saturn has helped rewrite industry rules on creating customer satisfaction and loyalty. In one national customer loyalty survey conducted for *Automotive News* and *Advertising Age*, Saturn ranked first in the eyes of customers for attentiveness and quality of customer contact. It also ranked first in terms of the likelihood of customers buying again from the same salesperson (Saturn calls them sales consultants) and from the same dealership (or retail facilities).[4] In the space of only five years, Saturn has established strong "brand equity," a marketplace perception of value anchored by a product name. It has also had a marked influence on the profile of the American car buying experience.

Saturn people talk naturally about delivering the "Saturn experience" for customers. The procedures for organizing that experience were deliberately planned and choreographed during "ramp-up," the phase in which Saturn and its new retail partners prepared to manufacture and market their cars. Saturn identified five core values it wanted to incorporate into every aspect of its business:

- Commitment to customer enthusiasm.
- Commitment to excel.
- Teamwork.
- Trust and respect for the individual.
- Continuous improvement.

Raising the Bar

From all accounts, Saturn and its retailers have been highly effective at demonstrating these values at the retail level. But they are also aware that the performance of retail employees—and how these values play out in the day-to-day business of selling and servicing cars—continues to evolve. This is true for two reasons.

In the first place, the blueprint for creating customer satisfaction was only recently just that: a paper plan devised by Saturn and its retailers to be a guide for serving customers and running a retail facility. Then, as Saturn retailers began the process of organizing their teams and as stores started to open, plans became reality. Predictably, much on-the-job learning has occurred since then regarding how best to apply retail guidelines. Today, the definition of effective practice—in conformance with the five core values—is naturally somewhat different than what the blueprint suggested it *might* look like.

The second reason why the profile of high performance continues to evolve at Saturn is that in redefining the car-buying experience, retailers also cause customers to readjust their expectations. In a sense, Saturn has helped contribute to a raising of the bar for retail automotive performance. To continue to create and sustain customer enthusiasm, it is necessary to continuously improve performance.

Revising the Blueprint

One strategy Saturn is using to help its retailers manage their business around the five core values is an organizational learning strategy. In fact, all of the core values—especially continuous improvement—are inherent to the motives of organizational learning. The strategy was initiated by Saturn's retail training group. It involves a systematic inquiry into the key behaviors, as defined by high-performing retail practitioners, for key job functions in the retail facility. What the inquiry is really about is finding usable answers to the following questions:

- What does high performance look like in actual practice? What do high performers do?
- How do high performance practices compare with existing performance standards and guidelines?
- What changes to high performance practices need to be made in light of new business plans?
- Where are the most significant gaps between high performance levels and the practices of the retail force at large?
- What are the factors that *enable* high performance practice, especially factors of individual competence and organizational support?

- What are the factors that *inhibit* high performance practice?
- What might be done to address enabling and inhibiting factors so as to improve retail performance?

Saturn's plan is to create a dialog around these questions with its retail partners. A series of facilitated group discussions are scheduled to focus on each of a dozen key roles. In all instances, two or more perspectives on each key role will be sought: those of the practitioners themselves, as well as the perspectives of their managers and either their direct reports or their customers. The insights gained from these conversations will then be pooled. While the main focus of discussion will be role-specific best practices, Saturn also expects to learn about how work processes and systems support high individual performance.

Additionally, Saturn's inquiry will turn outward, to include both other automotive practices, as well as best retail practices from non-automotive industries. What Saturn learns from this whole endeavor will be used most directly to guide the efforts of its retail training operations. More broadly, the organizational learning that takes place will help both Saturn and its retailers maintain their brand equity while continuing to enhance the customer experience.

CASE PROFILE

GEORGIA-PACIFIC

Increasingly, companies are seeking to improve their safety records by getting smarter about how to prevent accidents. At the heart of 22 recommendations generated at a convention of injury prevention and control specialists is an educational agenda: increasing company awareness and understanding of the "problem of preventable injuries and improving the information collection systems that will lead to other prevention techniques."[5]

Georgia-Pacific had good information on the most prevalent kinds of accidents occurring within their Building Products Division. Armed with this knowledge, company management decided to ask its employees to develop strategies that would reduce these accidents. An awareness campaign was launched to focus attention on the problem of preventable injuries. Literature on how to prevent eye and back injuries, and how to use power tools safely, was mailed to the *home*—another tactic to call attention to the seriousness of the problem.

Changing Learning into Habits

The real challenge, however, was to learn how to make safety behavior *habitual*. Georgia-Pacific chose to put this challenge to a rather large group of safety consultants: its employees. Learning how to make safety a habit, the company figured, is not something that management, or outside specialists, for that matter, really have a leg up on. So Georgia-Pacific turned to its own people. The company asked them to team up and teach each other to practice safety, to advise supervisors of unsafe working conditions, and to think of ways to make the workplace safer.

To reinforce this learning initiative, Georgia-Pacific did several things. They set accident reduction goals and measured progress against those goals on a monthly basis. They shared the results with everybody. And they also recognized plants and divisions for achieving their goals, with employees earning merchandise awards for their contributions to goal attainment.

Organizational learning aims to improve work performance and to accomplish a corporate mission. At Georgia-Pacific, reducing accidents and creating a safer work environment were part of an organizational learning mandate. At stake was not only the well-being and morale of the workforce, but the reduction of several financial consequences brought about by accidents on and off the job. The National Safety Council reports that over $100 billion in workers' compensation payments and system administration annual payments are paid out annually by American companies, making this a leading drain on corporate profits.

Georgia-Pacific's strategy of challenging its workforce to take charge in making safety a habit paid off in several ways. The health and welfare of 22,000 Building Products Division people, in more than 140 locations, were enhanced considerably. The company's OSHA recordable injury rate declined by 35.6 percent against the previous year. Two plants, in Cedar Springs, Georgia, and Emporia, Virginia, reported no lost-time accidents for the year.

Learning Partnerships

Georgia-Pacific presents an example of overcoming a blind spot regarding who knows best about an issue like safety improvement. As we saw in an earlier chapter, Georgia-Pacific has found that organizational learning works best when the whole organization is involved. When management challenges employees to think about improving business performance, it is shifting from a limiting bias to a liberating bias. Asking everyone to be a consultant creates a climate where knowledge building is valued, and where organizational learning is an expectation.

This trend towards getting beyond limiting biases extends outside the company as well. *Not invented here* is the traditional blind spot. Learning partnerships are the counter. Chrysler's approach to stepping around the not-invented-here barrier involves listening to its suppliers. As chairman Robert Eaton noted,

> It shouldn't surprise anybody that those who have the most to share with us are our own suppliers—the companies that provide 70 percent of what goes into the cars and trucks we sell. And yet, for years, we seldom asked them. We simply handed them specifications and gave the job to the lowest bidder.[6]

Now Chrysler and other automotives regularly share ideas with their suppliers and have come to expect this kind of cooperative learning as part of their relationship. Asking your supplier to suggest what process changes would help them to help you is a way to significantly cut costs and improve quality. Chrysler acknowledges having "received and implemented literally thousands of ideas from suppliers, which have saved us more than $400 million a year."[7]

Three-way learning partnerships can be observed in the energy industry. Duke Power and Florida Power, for instance, work with independent heating, ventilation, and air conditioning (HVAC) dealers to generate better profiles of residential and commercial energy users. Manufacturers of the equipment sold by these dealers also cooperate in building a more serviceable customer database. Combining market research with customer feedback from three different, but related, sources helps all of these enterprises better organize their resources and provide more on-target service.

In the following case, we'll see how another company enhanced organizational learning possibilities by enlisting wholesale partners to collaborate in improving performance.

CASE PROFILE

AMERITECH

An interesting trend among leading companies is to work closely with their distributors to develop "best practice" standards, and then to support improvement towards those standards. In so doing, each partner acknowledges that neither has a monopoly in defining best practices, and that different perspectives are valued.

Ameritech is one of the seven regional Bell holding companies that provide telecommunications products and related services. Ameritech sells its voice and data products to small and intermediate-size business clients through a network of over 200 distributors. In a highly fluid and competitive market, Ameritech must retain loyal and effective distributors. As a partnership, manufacturer and distributors are in a position to reinforce each other's growth and success—if they learn to work together well.

Ameritech has undertaken an ambitious effort to engage its distributors in a cooperative, business development process. For several years, Ameritech has invited representatives from its leading distributorships to discuss how they might improve the performance of their partnerships. The keynote for the process is the design of a comprehensive business building tool to focus improvement efforts on both long- and-short term results.

Developing the Business Building Tool

At their initial two-day meeting, the task force of Ameritech sales and marketing people and distributor representatives went through a structured exercise to establish a profile of the successful distribution operation. Their work was directed to accomplishing four objectives:

- Identify the activities and results that cause and indicate excellent performance.
- Establish an objective evaluation plan for measuring excellent performance.
- Prioritize and weight performance standards.
- Create an effective and consistent feedback system.

The exercise was facilitated by an outside firm. It involved painting a picture of operations "excellence," first with broad brush strokes, then with increasingly pinpointed detail. The task force agreed on five categories to organize their building of performance standards, or criteria: Sales and Marketing, Customer Service, Personnel and Training, Business Operations, and a final discretionary category that would be determined for each distributor by their Ameritech Distributor Manager.

With categories identified, the task force was asked to decide on how important each one was, relative to the others. The method used was to ask participants to divide 1,000 "points" among the categories, assigning appropriate point values to each. The discussion this step precipitates asks participants to think about what value different aspects of their operations bring to the business. The need to reach consensus forces them to test their views against one another.

Once the categories were established and weighted, the task force divided up into five subgroups, one per category. They would spend more than a day on the next task: determining specific performance criteria and measures for their respective categories that would guide performance improvement and serve as the basis to reward achievement. These sessions were sometimes arduous. Participants were taxed to get quite objective about their operations and to pinpoint actual *behaviors* whenever possible. The other discipline they worked through—fixing on the value of individual performance criteria—brought out still more strategic thinking, as well as some collective knowledge building.

The "customer service group," for instance, working with almost a quarter of the 1,000 points, came up with 12 criteria, divided among five headings. Under the heading of "Service Support," the group had five criteria. One, determined to be worth 10 points, said "Provides customers with live technical support during normal business hours." Another, also worth 10 points, reads "Maintains access to inventory of critical core products that allows for 'within 24–hour' equipment replacement in the event of failure." Almost all of the criteria were similarly anchored in behavioral terms, making for easy evaluation.

Growing the Partnership

Each year, Ameritech and its distributors revisit the criteria. Based on new business priorities and feedback on the tested validity of existing criteria, the task force can choose to change or reweight criteria. These annual sessions renew a business development practice where distributors and Ameritech staff collaborate on a continuous learning agenda. The outcome of the task force efforts is an ongoing reshaping of business operations and the relationship between business partners.

Ameritech's distributors are participating in a program that uses the "excellence criteria" to guide performance improvement efforts and to score performance to standards. Each year distributors that achieve a designated score are reinforced with award earning opportunities. Through the program, Ameritech is able to sponsor the dissemination of best practice guidelines across its network of distributors. The guidelines, plus the incentives, promote organizational learning activity in many different sites, which in turn channel feedback to Ameritech for use in future redesign efforts.

BEST PRACTICES AND BENCHMARKING

More and more, business organizations are recognizing that they have things to learn from one another. The growing occurrence of *benchmarking* best practices among different companies attests to our willingness to go beyond our own doors for new knowledge and insight.

Chrysler acknowledges in their annual report to stockholders that "We're not too proud to ask for help when we see somebody doing something better than we do it."

> We're learning a great deal from our own successes and our own false starts. . . . But we understand that our universe is limited, so we have people on airplanes almost every day, traveling to other companies to study the way those companies manage their processes. We're looking at the best practices of the best companies all over the world, and if they make sense for us, we're adopting them. The old "not invented here" syndrome is not appreciated at Chrysler.[8]

While we'll not go too deeply into benchmarking in this book, most companies we know that have used benchmarking to good learning advantage tend to follow these guidelines:

1. Target specific functions or processes to study.
2. Determine key variables in the processes.
3. Identify companies that offer best-in-class, or interesting alternative, approaches.
4. Determine study strategy and collect data.
5. Compare and discuss implications of findings.

A benchmarking initiative is like an "action learning" exercise. It begins with a focus, proceeds with some discoveries, and concludes with reflection on what was seen and what might be done. If the data that are collected and the observations that are made can be widely shared, then the learning potential to be derived from benchmarking is, of course, expanded.

OPPORTUNISM: OUTSIDE-IN AND BOTTOM-UP

Companies that engage their business partners—their trade allies, their distributors, their suppliers—in a process of knowledge building are leveraging organizational learning. They are declaring that they can indeed benefit from other perspectives, other points of view. They are also acknowledging that their own views are not necessarily definitive or even always reliable. This kind of collaborative knowledge building can contribute mightily to the exposure and resolution of contradictory, nonproductive thinking. It dissolves blind spots.

Similarly, companies that welcome thoughtful input from employees whose expertise is neither credentialed (as with process engineers or safety experts, say), nor "titled" (as with managers), are companies that are engaging an available, but underused, consultancy. *To recognize this source of organizational learning is a first step.* To facilitate employee problem solving and innovation is more difficult, but clearly worth the effort. Without effective communication and reinforcement, this latent consultancy will remain latent.

The cases we looked at above offered examples of how to support knowledge building from two different sources: outside-in and bottom-up. When companies are able to tap these two sources, they are at the same time reducing the impact of some of the blind spots that inhibit progress and change. And these two sources of organizational learning are clearly sources of competitive advantage.

Chapter Seven

Using Feedback

Feedback is the breakfast of champions.

Anonymous

When work teams don't debrief on completed projects, they may in fact be subtly shielding themselves, and their managers, from potentially irksome findings. When managers ignore or don't follow through on customer research, they might be indirect participants in a practice of collusion to maintain a positive front at all costs. And when companies routinely discourage negative criticism, they may be indirectly conferring more value on people's feelings than on the legitimate needs of the organization. In all these cases, the habit of wearing "rose-colored glasses" prevents people in companies from *learning from their experience*.

The strategy for countering this tendency starts with a companywide acknowledgement that regular, unvarnished feedback is a *requirement* for success. If news is bad, we don't hide (or hide from) it. We learn from it. Messengers don't get shot. They get encouraged and reinforced. Companies seek to make feedback both systematic and routine. Securing and disseminating feedback becomes the expected way of doing business. In the following case profiles, we'll examine several different attempts at formalizing opportunities to learn from feedback.

CASE PROFILE

FORD

Ford plant operations have a catchall term for vehicle defects and problems: TGWs. TGWs stands for "things gone wrong." Most TGWs are noticed before vehicles leave the assembly plant. But those that aren't, or those that happen somewhere between the plant and the point of sale—while vehicles are in transit—are usually caught as part of the "predelivery inspection." The predelivery inspection is a standard routine in which the dealer begins to ready the car for sale. What the dealer does about notifying Ford regarding discovered defects is, in part, an issue of how—and whether—to deliver "bad news."

Two things are at stake for Ford in this decision. First and foremost is taking care of customers and their cars. But Ford also has an opportunity here to quickly reengineer "fixes" into the assembly or transportation processes so as to prevent continued TGWs. If the dealers feel that reporting defects is an invitation to "shoot the messenger," or is simply more trouble than it's worth, a valuable learning opportunity is denied to Ford.

Company-to-Dealer Standards

As part of its "Quality Is Job 1" policy, Ford had established quality standards to define both its own products and the service it wanted its dealers to extend to customers throughout the ownership experience. In cooperation with its dealers, Ford later created an additional set of standards to improve quality levels in the sales and service support Ford provides to its dealers. These were called Company-to-Dealer Standards. Company-to-Dealer Quality Standard #2 states that "all vehicles will be delivered to the dealer in proper working order, with no defects."

Ford engineering has always been responsible for designing out defects, and correcting factors that cause defects, in production processes. But Ford thought that engineers might be assisted in spotting problems by those dealer personnel assigned the task of receiving vehicle shipments and preparing them for delivery to customers. The idea was that by working together, plant and dealerships could move the needle on Standard #2 in several ways:

- Identifying and resolving specific product concerns.
- Developing product improvements.
- Identifying and implementing process improvements.

Ford invited its dealerships to participate in this quality improvement initiative by checking out each newly received vehicle, completing a form on each one, and sending the forms back to Ford within 48 hours of delivery. "Dealer prep" teams were also invited to make suggestions on how specific problems might be solved. Ford's intention was to enlist the dealerships as quality control partners. Prompt feedback from the dealer prep teams would enable Ford to design in corrective action and prevent future problems.

Helping Communication Happen

In the normal scheme of things, plant engineers don't talk with dealer service personnel. Dealer prep teams, however, were in a unique position to provide useful feedback to the plants about the condition of cars that were being readied for sale. And when someone on the dealer prep team needed to report a problem in any detail, it would help if he could communicate directly with the plant. Another key to making feedback as accurate and as thorough as possible was to establish the checkout procedure, with its reporting form, as the critical communication between *partners* in the car delivery process.

To facilitate this kind of cooperation, Ford recognized it needed to open up lines of communication between the factory and the dealership. Dealer representatives had to feel that their input was welcomed and valued. And plant engineers, product designers, and quality team members needed to feel comfortable in accepting input from their retail partners. This could be a challenge, as the following comments by a Ford project manager attest:

> Most engineers are afraid to admit they have a problem. They fear people will think they don't know how to do their job, and they dread interference from others who think they know the answer.[1]

For starters, Ford decided to bring together dealer and plant representatives to meet face to face. The visits would actually serve several purposes: to help partners get to know one another, to help dealer people develop a better understanding of production processes at the plant, and to establish some agreed upon protocols for reporting issues to plant quality teams.

The two-day visits have turned into highly successful exercises in organizational learning. The routine typically begins with a tour of the plant. For most dealer people, this has been a significant learning experience in itself. One dealer shop foreman admitted that he'd been in the business for 30 years, and this was his first visit to a plant. "I've really changed my perspective on manufacturing. I now understand the challenges of assembly line employees and why certain defects occur."

After the tour, dealer representatives receive some training on the diagnostic process. Then they break into teams and are given the opportunity to check for defects on two demonstration vehicles. They record their findings, and present them to the rest of the group. This practice exercise, followed by group discussion, provides a kind of rehearsal for both the check-out procedure, and the quality circle process that will be taken up again at the next plant visit.

About six months later, the dealer representatives pay their second visit to the plant. This time they meet in small, cross-functional groups (quality circles) to discuss process issues. The goal of these sessions is to build the capability of the participants to function effectively as problem spotting, problem solving teams. Toward the close of the second day, the small groups come together and report to everyone on key concerns and how they might be resolved.

Afterwards, Ford disseminates the knowledge generated in the group sessions throughout the organization in an attractive newsletter. The newsletter also recognizes specific accomplishments and the people who were responsible. Ford provides further assistance to dealers in the form of training packets for use in building an efficient delivery inspection routine.

So far, the dealer prep teams are providing considerable feedback that plant engineers can use to design permanent fixes for improved quality. Plant personnel seem delighted to learn from their partners in the field, as these accounts from plants in Ohio and Michigan, reported in issues of Ford's *Update* newsletter, attest.

- We've been able to make major improvements with seat rattles, rear suspension noises, adjustments in the flip glass, and left door glass weatherstripping. When we got reports of rattles in the sliding doors, we made adjustments on the line to eliminate the problem and then sent people to the dealerships to instruct them in how to adjust the doors to eliminate customer complaints. We use the reports religiously at the plant.

- We rely heavily on the dealers for information. They give us a lot of feedback and help us out a lot. . . . The face to face communication is very helpful. We get the chance to express our feelings that we really want their data; that we need more specific data to help us better to identify problems. And they were saying, "Yes, we understand better now." That really makes it worthwhile.

- We reengineered the carpet to make it fit better around the accelerator pedal, under the rear seat, and on the convertibles on the side retractor belt, because we're listening to Standard #2. I personally went to South Carolina where they make the carpet and got with the supplier and we sat down and redesigned the carpet to what the dealers were telling us.

When dealer prep teams go over newly received cars and trucks, they're looking for any TGWs they might report to Ford. But from time to time, dealer technicians will also make suggestions that result in process changes and fixes being implemented at the assembly plant.

Checkout forms for one Ford vehicle were reporting bulges in the carpet on the interior of a door. A parts and service director from a dealership in Maryland suggested adding a strip of glue along the edge of the carpet at the door, which they were doing in their own shop to fix the problem. After Ford engineers reviewed this idea, they decided to adopt the process at the plant, and it has since been put into operation on the assembly line.

What Ford has accomplished in this exercise of active collaboration between plant and dealerships goes beyond the improvements to Ford products. Giving feedback is often more complicated than just presenting information to another party. Ford realized that in this situation, the process of feedback itself needed to be reengineered. The results can now be measured in organizational learning achievements, from which Ford will continue to reap dividends.

CASE PROFILE

TIG INSURANCE

Formerly Transamerica Insurance Group, TIG Insurance is a company that has prided itself on being lean at the top. But to be lean at the top means you have to have well-organized, more self-directed work processes below. TIG Insurance has worked to build such an organization by emphasizing teams, continuous improvement, and feedback.

In the last decade, the insurance industry has seen considerable process reengineering to improve operations quality and productivity. Stiff price competition is one of the market conditions forcing this need to manage work more efficiently. TIG Insurance had embraced total quality as a logical strategy to use. But after establishing hundreds of productivity and quality measures, the company had little improvement to show for its effort. The approach TIG eventually found to produce results (with two-thirds of the more than 300 measures reflecting dramatic improvement) was one that understood the importance of feedback, learning, and reinforcement.

Teams, Measures, Feedback, Rewards

With an initiative it called "Stretch for Success," TIG Insurance attempted to use targeted work process measures to energize performance improvement in key departments. Natural work groups at department levels—including administration and operations, underwriting, marketing, and claims—focused on a specific range of corporate objectives. Measures would be identified as a source of performance feedback for each work group, or team. Teams were accountable for performance goals that they could impact, and for which they could receive clear and regular feedback. Teams would also earn awards for goal attainment, with the top performing teams earning an additional, special award.

A TIG Insurance planning task force followed these steps in putting Stretch for Success together:

1. Identify teams by facility location and by job function.
2. Establish three to five measures, specific to their work product, for each team.
   - Not all teams have the same number of measures, but
   - Similar teams have identical measures.
   - Frequency varies according to measures (i.e., monthly, quarterly, semiannually).
3. Target baselines and goals for each measure.
   - Derived from historical performance and corporate standards
   - Developed with manager's participation
   - Personalized to each team
4. Develop matrix award system.
   - Weighted by service level and dollar impact
   - Weighted by difficulty of attainment

Baselines were defined as the level of performance TIG Insurance was trying to improve upon. Typically, baselines were derived from average performance over the latest 12 month period. TIG Insurance also prepared team leaders to assist their teams in understanding both baselines and their rationale. The process of using performance measures to assess improvement over baselines helped teams extend their awareness of company priorities, as well as their understanding of how productivity impacts business success.

Richard Wratten, then president of the Commercial Insurance Division, noted several other organizational learning benefits. First of all, the effort forced senior management to establish a more comprehensive set of criteria that could be used to measure the performance of operating units. Furthermore, the management information that Stretch for Success generated enabled TIG Insurance to more easily spot trends. "For example, if our Intermountain Region in Arizona scored "fours" (on a 1–5 scale) on a given criterion and our Southern California Region scored zero on the same criterion, we knew we had a localized problem. If all our regions scored low on a given criterion, it suggested a shift in the competitive or economic environment, and may have begged a possible strategic action."[2]

TIG Insurance's experience with measurement-driven performance improvement, where work teams concentrate on moving a few key indicators that they control, produced substantial productivity gains. It also resulted in the workforce getting smarter about how to run the business.

Training Derived from Research

Customer research captures the "voice of the customer." But sometimes this voice *remains* the captive of a select few, often those who commissioned the research and who choose to restrict the audience that will see the findings. In the two cases that follow, we'll look at examples of companies doing just the opposite. They recognized that customer research needs to be shared broadly within their organizations and, most important, with those people who can best act on the findings. Because they saw the learning potential in their research investment, they opted to leverage that investment through specially targeted training programs.

CASE PROFILE

BUDGET RENT-A-CAR

Budget Rent-A-Car recognizes how important customer service is in a business where all of the competitors basically rent the same product. To learn more about what its customers found most positive in dealing with vehicle rental companies, as well as what turned them off, Budget undertook an intensive series of focus groups and interviews with both customers and employees. They recorded many of the views they gathered on videotape.

But Budget wanted to do more than gather points of view. They realized that the best way to prepare their workforce to deliver the right kind of service was to give them all the opportunity to hear what was on customers' minds. The interview tapes therefore became the subject matter for a series of training programs aimed at developing more effective ways to manage the "moments of truth" for Budget customers.

For most customers, there are two obvious, critical moments of truth when dealing with vehicle rentals. The first is securing the vehicle, and the second is returning it. Depending on the circumstances, both can be either routine and straightforward or frustrating and stressful. For employees, the experience of listening to customers describe what they feel when they rush to catch a plane and encounter a line at the rental counter has the potential to heighten empathy for the customer. And empathy is the stuff on which we can build more effective service strategies.

Budget also taped observations made by veteran staff concerning varieties of customer behavior they've encountered. One called attention to how certain types of customers who've just arrived at an unfamiliar airport, and now face the drill of renting a car, can act as if they "left their brain at home before boarding the plane." They're confused by what seems to others to be the simplest of routines. But armed with this insight about the state of mind some customers can understandably be in, a Budget employee has an opportunity to turn a moment of truth into a positive transaction.

Budget has found that this kind of vivid depiction of customer expectations and customer impressions has a powerful impact on learning. Employees process what they see and hear and come up with their own ideas for handling moments of truth. What began as an effort to learn about customers has become, through the most logical of steps, an effective dissemination strategy and a prompt for knowledge creating activity across the company.

CASE PROFILE

AMERICAN EXPRESS FINANCIAL ADVISORS

American Express Financial Advisors (formerly IDS) presents another case where client feedback is deployed in a creative way for performance improvement purposes. A major business development strategy is to improve customer satisfaction levels for its financial services product line. American Express has found that almost two of every five clients it loses cite factors related to financial advisor service as the main reason.

Financial advisors are located in independent offices across the country. Advisors *are* the company for their clients. They must perform a variety of functions and require a versatile set of competencies to deliver their services well. American Express Financial Advisors has identified seven key client expectations that define good service. To improve satisfaction levels, the company endeavors to collect client reactions to the services they receive and provides that feedback to advisors. The company then asks its advisors to act to close any gaps between expectations and service delivery.

Getting the Message

American Express Financial Advisors has for some time surveyed clients and passed findings along to the advisors. The company was aware, however, that this attempt at providing performance feedback was not having much of an impact. Overall, advisors were somewhat skeptical and did not put much value in the survey. For whatever reasons, the "voice of the customer" was not registering as a direction for performance improvement.

A new approach was needed. American Express Financial Advisors decided to regard the whole process of surveying clients and using the findings to improve service levels as more of a learning experience. Thus reframed, the process required a shifting and an expansion of its objectives.

Learning objectives for the advisors

- Understand the value of the Client Satisfaction Survey (CSS) process.
- Interpret their individual CSS scores.
- Draw a relationship between their CSS results and specific service behaviors.
- Identify areas for improvement in their client interactions.
- Develop a behavior-specific action plan to enhance client service.

The process also needed to be engaged with differently by financial advisors. To accomplish this, American Express Financial Advisors worked to make the information delivered to advisors more user friendly. Individual results for each of the seven performance categories are provided separately on a diskette. The diskette shows individual scores compared to district and division averages, presented as colored bar graphs. The diskette is actually read "through" a CD-ROM learning program that helps advisors understand the potential of the CSS as a business building tool. The course also assists advisors in interpreting their scores.

Most importantly, though, the learning program helps advisors make decisions about performance shortfalls and how to strategize for improvement. Each of the seven performance categories is represented by a segment featuring a mentor, a high-performing advisor who addresses that particular subject. Advisors using the program can engage in a strategy development dialog about performance areas that they want to work on.

American Express Financial Advisors has enlarged upon its investment in customer research to make sure that useful learning actually occurs. They've approached feedback as an important learning tool, but one which needs to be understood in the context of user reluctance to heed its findings.

TAKING OFF THE ROSE-COLORED GLASSES

In each of the four cases above, a company was able to counteract the natural tendencies of its people to avoid or ignore critical information that might indeed be somehow critical of them. Each of these companies demonstrated an abiding commitment not only to seek feedback to guide future action, but to mine that feedback for its maximum organizational learning potential. Each of these companies also recognized that real barriers stood in the way of learning from feedback. When feedback is delayed or degraded, there are significant consequences for performance improvement.

In research conducted for the Conference Board, HR executives were surveyed about factors they felt affected work performance in their companies. The respondents were asked to indicate which of a list of "causative factors" that can influence performance improvement would elicit high performance from their workforce. They were also asked to identify causes of deficient performance.

"Data, information, feedback" was the category that ranked fourth among the primary causes of *high* performance (behind "skills and knowledge," "individual capacity," and "motives and expectations"). And among the primary causes of *deficient* performance, "poor or insufficient performance feedback" ranked first (identified by 60 percent of the respondents; the next cause was "high individual stress levels," named by 40 percent of respondents).[3] There are, to be sure, many reasons why feedback may be poor or insufficient. But for both *the source* and *the receiver* of feedback, there need to be clear and compelling (as well as compensatory) reasons for this tool to be well-used.

Chapter Eight

Adjusting Focus

Market orientation is the foundation of the learning organization.

Slater and Narver[1]

Organizational learning is about being competent to succeed in the future. It aims to prepare the organization to work effectively both in the short and the long term. When a company does not make an effort to look beyond its present products or services, it risks being left behind by changes in market demand. If an organization is too busy filling present orders to be inquiring what else its customers might want, it can miss opportunities to add value—and profit—from new business. And if a company does not make a deliberate and consistent effort to stay in touch with customers, it will miss the critical signals that provide direction into the future.

The corporate vision problem of *myopia* is really a failure to keep the marketplace—and the customer—clearly in sight. It is a failure to keep one's bearings. It's akin to focusing only on the ship and not on the sea, and to ignore the navigational cues that can keep us from losing our way. Companies that don't lose their way are commited to actively scanning their environment. They focus their attention on demographic, technological, and regulatory trends. But they also work to understand those trends, so that they might extract some business advantage from them.

The cases we'll consider in this chapter show companies aligning their focus on the customer. They also show companies doing more than just listening and observing. The cases illustrate in addition how organizations can derive real learning dividends from the ways they respond to , and act on, information from customers. They depict companies engaged in turning information about customers and the marketplace into knowledge that adds value to their business.

CASE PROFILE

WENDY'S

In the highly competitive fast food industry, pleasing customers takes on added significance as companies strive to attract and hold a clientele. Wendy's, like its competition, has surveyed customers to determine what they value and how well the stores were seen to provide what customers want. Focus groups had been used to get deeper into issues and to test new product ideas. But the company acknowledged that it could also benefit from a different kind of conversation with its customers.

What Wendy's had in mind was an opportunity to engage its customers in a more consultative role. Rather than ask customers to point out problems or dislikes, Wendy's would, for a change, seek some input on *solutions*. How would customers design different aspects of the restaurant experience so that it would meet a variety of expectations and provide the most desirable kind of service?

The plan the company ultimately devised wound up extending to Wendy's store employees and headquarters staff as well. All three groups were, in different ways, stakeholders in the successful operation of the Wendy's restaurant business. The strategy was therefore to ask each kind of stakeholder to become, for half a day, "virtual partners" in the business. Their challenge was to develop recommendations for making business better.

Thinking Like Virtual Partners

Groups representing each of these three constituencies were convened as a kind of planning task force. The pretext: imagine you're part of a family who had just inherited a fast food chain. At your first board of directors meeting, you need to address a specific side of restaurant business—the drive-through operation.

The group sessions were facilitated, and participants were helped to build their recommendations with some creative thinking techniques. Their first objective was to generate a lot of ideas. Several tactics designed to get beyond more conventional, patterned thinking were introduced by the facilitator. Once idea lists were created, the groups were asked to remember that they were, indeed, "owners" and that they now needed to make some feasibility decisions regarding those ideas. The ensuing discussion resulted in tossing out some ideas, and combining others, so that a much more manageable list remained. A final step involved a priority-setting exercise, which brought the list of ideas even closer to the status of an action plan.

The sessions produced both insights about customer preferences and practical suggestions for improvement. Discussion ranged over many aspects of the operation: Food preparation, customer handling, ergonomics, and what customers might do while they waited were only a few. Wendy's came away with a feeling that they had learned some things from all three stakeholders that could add value to store operations. They also knew that they had tapped into their customers' thinking in a rather unprecedented way.

CASE PROFILE

FORT SANDERS HEALTH SYSTEM

Fort Sanders Health System, headquartered in Knoxville, Tennessee, is an integrated health services system employing about 5,000 people. The Fort Sanders mission statement is "We are an alliance of people and organizations with a common dedication to serve the people of East Tennessee as the area's preeminent health care provider." Fort Sanders employees wear badges that proclaim a Quality Vision: "We share a genuine commitment to combine our individual talents and services to meet or exceed the identified needs and expectations of our customers."

Clearly, Fort Sanders sees itself as an organization making common cause, in part by combining and integrating its many resources. Fort Sanders also has demonstrated a strong bias toward learning partnerships, involving both its customers and its employees. Learning is the foundation for its continuous quality improvement (CQI) process. The learning takes place in a variety of ways, several of which are deliberately orchestrated.

Customer research, at the heart of the Fort Sanders CQI model, is a major source of learning and knowledge building. For healthcare providers, there are actually two kinds of customers: internal and external. Patients, of course, are one. But there are also the physicians who refer patients to hospitals. Fort Sanders initiated its customer research with focus groups involving not only patients (with their families) and physicians, but employees as well.

The focus groups gave Fort Sanders a clearer idea about what their customers felt were the most important "satisfiers" in their dealings with the system. What did physicians value most? What were the highest priority service expectations held by patients? What did employees think mattered the most—both for themselves and for customers? Were there gaps between customer and employee perceptions of satisfaction?

From the focus group findings, a questionnaire of approximately 40 satisfaction factors was designed. It is administered by telephone on a schedule to 225 patients. Baseline satisfaction measurements were established early, and ongoing quarterly reports reflect changes compared to the baselines. One of the research interpretation tools used by Fort Sanders is called the *Performance Improvement Planner*. The planner, shown opposite, enables Fort Sanders leadership to sort the findings according to two criteria: how important each factor is to the customer and how well that factor is being delivered.

The planner allows Fort Sanders to plot findings from its customer research so as to determine which ones to act upon, and in what order of priority. Service issues determined to be of relatively high importance to customers are collected within the top two quadrants. Issues in the top right quadrant are those which deserve attention because they're important, but more in a maintenance mode, because they are currently well-performed. Issues

PERFORMANCE IMPROVEMENT PLANNER

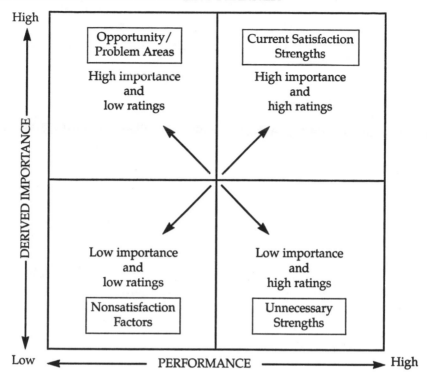

in the top left quadrant represent the biggest opportunity for improving satisfaction levels: They're important, and there's a gap between expectation and actual delivery that needs to be closed.

Issues that cluster below the line, indicating lesser importance to the customer, are not necessarily to be ignored. Underperformance here can still prompt corrective action, but it is of lower priority. For items below the line that are perceived as well-performed, there may be reason to examine whether too much investment is being made here, possibly at the expense of items that need improvement.

The primary usage of the performance planner is, of course, to identify and prioritize service gaps. But teams can also use it as a way to organize their thinking for new services or extensions of existing service.

Building a Learning Climate

Fort Sanders had earlier implemented a strong team-based program, called Team Alliance, to generate savings and revenue ideas. Eighty-seven percent of the system's employees participated. More than 2,100 ideas were submitted, and bottom line results exceeded $3 million. The team experience had also fired up the engines for more problem solving and knowledge building. In addition to achieving the targeted levels of cost savings and new revenues, Team Alliance helped prepare the ground for an aggressive continuous quality improvement focus systemwide.

Team Alliance, a short-term initiative, has thus been succeeded by Quality Alliance, Fort Sanders' ongoing CQI process. Teams are still a central part of the knowledge building strategy. Team facilitators, key members of the CQI infrastructure, are drawn from the ranks of managers and staff and take part in specially designed training. The curriculum includes an orientation to the CQI process and topics like teamwork, process management, transformational leadership, and creative thinking tactics. The latter is covered through a course developed by the Center for Creative Leadership called *Targeted Innovation.*

Learning from Customer Research

With a mandate to question established routines and training that supports the creation of better alternatives, teams and individuals at Fort Sanders are well-positioned to use customer research to good advantage. Highlights from the quarterly reports provide useful input for CQI teams, as well as for individuals. Research can identify performance gaps in need of attention, and project teams can be directed accordingly. But in other cases, it is simply the heightened awareness of what customers want and value that enables teams to come up with new ways of thinking about health care quality.

Ellen Kidd is the vice president of CQI at Fort Sanders. She sees the use of customer research as a key part of the CQI strategy:

> We feel like we're starting up front with the emphasis on the customer. By looking at it that way and concentrating our efforts on what seems to be the top priority, CQI is more focused. The areas that need atten-

tion receive it first. Once the customers are satisfied, then the bottom line tends to follow.[2]

Fort Sanders is commited not only to listening to the voice of the customer, but also to reflecting on what can be done and then taking action to make health care better. They're getting a real return on their customer research because they are proactive about learning from information and commited to improvement and change. And, they're benefiting from deploying *teams* to work on the implications of customer research because teams can get things done.

PROFILING THE CUSTOMER

From the standpoint of organizational learning, keeping in touch with customer needs and expectations is certainly a logical starting point. Besides customer opinion surveys, as used by organizations like Fort Sanders, there are a growing number of tools that offer insights into customer buying behavior and how to align with it. Database marketing, for instance, collects detailed marketing information about existing customers that can serve as the basis for rethinking how better to meet their needs.

Companies like Anheuser Busch and AT&T Universal Card that maintain state-of-the-art call centers (or "customer relations centers") have a built-in capability to broaden and enrich their customer databases. Handling inbound calls, be they requests for information or complaints about service, provides access to new information that can be used to fill out a customer profile. Trend data obtained by monitoring inbound calls can also be a source for spotting potential problems or potential opportunities. Changes in buying habits or usage patterns become prompts for reflection on how the business might reassess its products and services.

The organizational learning challenge for companies with increased access to customer information lies in turning information into knowledge. Most of the literature sees this as a challenge for management. We see it equally as an opportunity *to energize and inform the work of employee teams.* Building on information to renew business practices for the future is as much a bottom-up enterprise as it is a top management expectation. Sometimes, it works better from the bottom up.

A GLOSS ON CUSTOMER RESEARCH

Companies that attempt to really learn from customer research typically acknowledge the need to consider "internal" as well as external customers. They also recognize that research findings by themselves do not necessarily produce insights that lead to performance improvement. Gouillart and Sturdivant give this useful counsel on how to learn from customers:

1. Recognize that "customer" means more than the next step in the distribution chain.
2. Count on your customers for information, not for insight.
3. Don't expect to take each insight about customers to the bank.
4. Involve all levels of the organization in the effort to learn from customers. [3]

The value that customer research holds for organizational learning needs also to be considered in the light of three other factors. First, there's a **time lag factor,** which implies that the longer a company takes in disseminating or acting on research findings, the more unreliable, and the less useful, they become. Stale information about customers can sometimes be more misleading than enlightening.

There is also what we'll call a **filter factor** that acts in much the same way that rose-colored glasses do to water down or distort communications. When companies don't disseminate customer research findings or distill them to the extent that they lose their impact and their power to instruct, they undercut the potential learning return on their research investment.

Finally, there is an **over reliance factor,** which works on the assumption that the needs of customers are independent givens that companies merely try to respond to. The implication here is that all we need to do is to stay close to customers, understand their requirements, and fulfill them. But such an assumption exemplifies what Hamel and Prahalad call "the tyranny of the served market." Rather than just do research with customers, they suggest that companies need to study non-customers as well.[4]

Organizational learning is best served when we regard the market as an open, dynamic situation, rather than as static and stable. Relying too heavily on customer research is to ignore the *interdependency* of seller and buyer and the power of the seller to create demand, to invent products and services that buyers will discover a need for. Organizational learning starts with the customer in mind, but is not limited to existing customer expectations or even existing customers.

Chapter Nine

Taking Risks

The more leaders clarify the company's intentions and ground rules, the more people will be able to predict and influence what happens to them—even in the middle of a constantly shifting situation.

Jeanie Daniel Duck[1]

When fear inhibits risk taking and innovation, it acts as a barrier to organizational learning. The sources of fear can be *internal*, as when we avoid trying new tasks because we don't want to fail. Or they can be *external*, as in situations where mistakes are punished or where job loss is a potential reality. In this chapter we'll look at two companies in transition that worked successfully to minimize the impact of fear on learning and positive change.

STEPPING OUT

The anxiety that attaches to trying new things, learning different routines, and assuming strange and unfamiliar roles, is a natural accompaniment to change. But if this anxiety is shared by large groups of workers, even departments and divisions, it can paralyze the learning efforts necessary to adapt to change. Such anxiety and fear of failing can create chronic dependency relationships upon management. These in turn can effectively neutralize the power of a workforce to contribute much in the way of added value to an evolving business.

In this section, we'll consider how a company in transition sought to energize its workforce and summon new initiatives to keep pace with changing market and regulatory conditions. We'll examine the approaches this company took to refocus its people on a new business agenda. And we'll review how one particular strategy—*reinforcement and reward systems*—became the means for rededicating its people to new corporate goals and new corporate values.

CASE PROFILE

AT&T

As postdivestiture, deregulated AT&T sought to reshape its mission and its operations, it found itself caught up in a process of major business and cultural change. One dimension of this change involved internal support divisions and their relationships with the line operations. In the new business climate, AT&T needed to adopt a more competitive posture, and everyone in the organization needed to align with that stance.

As a consequence, certain internal support functions would no longer be the automatic choice to provide services to AT&T's widespread operating divisions. Operating units would henceforth be able to shop for these services. Thus some support divisions found *themselves* in a competitive situation whereas before they had enjoyed a virtual monopoly. Their employees would be charged with new marketplace accountabilities and asked to assume roles that many of them had never been asked to take on before.

Building a Strategy for Change

AT&T faced a formidable challenge: It was basically being tasked to change its character, to become a different kind of organization. It needed to engineer and carry through a shift.

From:	To:
A stable (but apprehensive) workforce identifying with department and function, and with these characteristics:	A proactive, motivated workforce with a marketing mindset, and with these characteristics:
• Internal focus.	• External focus.
• Operations orientation.	• Customer orientation.
• Budget driven.	• Profit driven.
• Conservative, risk averse.	• Entrepreneurial, innovative.
• Bureaucratic, decision by consensus.	• Decisive, flexible, fast moving.

Senior managers in one internal support division understood that this shift involved more than restructuring and the reengineering of work processes. They recognized that the organization itself needed to change its sense of priorities, its work habits, and its culture. They therefore set about to study present work orientations and the support structures that underpinned and reinforced those orientations. Their approach was to let this analysis identify the best change targets and guide appropriate change strategies. The study phase of this initiative focused on three areas: *culture, rewards,* and *performance measurements.*

Cultural Audit

Because of its reconfigured business environment, AT&T had already developed a new platform of corporate goals and corporate values to guide the company's operations. The support division would need to work from that platform too. To determine how much in sync its organization was with the new business platform, the division commissioned a cultural audit. The audit would yield a clearer sense of how strongly held, and how widely shared, the new values were within the division. It would therefore yield a picture of how well aligned the division was with the new mission and values.

The division based its study on a descriptive model of "human resource cultures" developed by Sethia and Von Glinow.[2] The model defined culture according to two different value orientations: concern for people and concern for organizational performance. The division adapted the model slightly and called it their "Motivational Model of Organizational Culture."

The Motivational Model of Culture

	High	Caring/Paternalistic	Integrative/Involving
		• Compliance	• Innovation
		• Cooperation	• Cooperation
		• Policies	• Risk Taking
Concern		• Tenure	• Group Performance
for		Apathetic	Exacting/Demanding
People		• Politicking	• Efficiency
		• Perception	• Competition
		• Anecdotes	• Individual Performance
		• Contract	• Job Position
	Low		High

Concern for Organization Performance Improvement

The findings of the cultural audit described a culture in flux. The large majority of human resource practices, as well as other aspects of its organizational climate, identified the division's prevailing orientation to be "Caring/Paternalistic," located in the upper left quadrant of the model. Qualities of a "Caring" culture include high concern for the comfort and well-being of its people, but with less regard to how they contributed to the success of the enterprise. Emphasis is on compliance with policies and informal work rules.

The cultural orientation that AT&T now viewed as being most appropriate to its new business goals and organizational values was "Integrative/High Involvement," located in the upper right quadrant. This orientation holds that people are capable of working together to contribute significantly to the overall goals of the company. It acknowledges risk taking and innovation to be ingredients of significant contributions. It is also, by implication, the orientation that is most likely to support organizational learning.

Measurement Audit

The division was also interested in determining how its family of performance measurements aligned with its new business goals and values. Here the study examined a range of measurements, from financial and customer satisfaction indicators to team and individual performance measures. In addition, the division wanted to find out how ably its measurements could support an effective motivation strategy. The study used an instrument that assessed conformance to 11 separate performance measurement attributes.

Study findings showed that the division did indeed have adequate and appropriate measures in place. Most interviewees were familiar with the measures and their importance, although there was some uncertainty about relative importance of different measures. The study also indicated that the actual deployment of measures, and their use for performance feedback and learning, could be improved.

Reinforcement Audit

The division recognized that its reward systems were a key strategy for defining the new culture, shaping new behaviors, and reinforcing higher levels of achievement. In order to assess the ways in which existing reward systems could support the new business goals and reflect the new corporate values, the division conducted interviews and focus groups with both human resource managers and line managers and employees. The basis for the questions used in the research was a Reward System Effectiveness Model, developed by Maritz Performance Improvement.

The Reward System Effectiveness Model is founded on two principles:

- **Reward systems must have** *direction:* they need to be aligned with desired values and business objectives.
- **Reward systems must have** *power:* they must possess certain key attributes to assure maximum impact.

REWARD SYSTEM EFFECTIVENESS MODEL

Direction × Power = Effectiveness

DIRECTION: aligned with . . .
- desired cultural values.
- business goals and objectives.

POWER: possessing . . .
- top-of-mind awareness.
- perceived value to employee.
- performance sensitivity.

Reward systems are effective to the extent they support behaviors that contribute to the achievement of business goals and objectives. *Direction* addresses this issue of alignment. Somewhat surprisingly, many organizations have reward systems in place that are partially misaligned. The consequences of misalignment include a lessened return on their reward system investment and a compromise to organizational learning efforts.

The *power* of reward systems is a function of the impact they have on shaping and reinforcing behavior. In order to be influenced by a reward system, employees must first be fully aware of it. Second, they need to perceive that the rewards which can be attained are worth the effort required. Third, they must feel that there is a direct and fairly managed cause and effect connection between effort made and the attainment of reward.

At AT&T, reward systems needed to reinforce the behaviors characteristic of an "Integrative/High Involvement" business culture. What the internal support division found from its reinforcement audit was that most reward systems were not perceived to be strongly linked to AT&T's new corporate goals. Overall, the attributes of existing reward and support systems tended to reinforce the behaviors of the *Caring* cultural orientation. In particular, risk taking was not encouraged by existing reward systems.

Leading Change

The division understood how reward systems can communicate what's important and emphasize the right things to do in the work process. It also realized that it was not leveraging its current reward systems to maximize performance return. The division wanted to *lead* change, not simply react to it. A major strategy for leading change was to actively support and reinforce desired new behaviors.

The division wanted its employees venturing confidently into the new business environment, offering the most competitive customer service and learning new roles and responsibilities. To accomplish all this, it would have to develop and implement properly aligned reinforcement strategies. Supervisory managers were therefore asked to identify key performance indicators for their work groups, in the context of the division's new business mission. They were also asked to design appropriate reward systems for their people, using the Reward System Effectiveness Model as their guide.

To become a more entrepreneurial, innovative service organization when neither of these attributes was a particularly high priority for internal support divisions in the past meant reinventing the organization. It meant risking failure for some who never had to take that kind of risk in the workplace before. The division moved forward by fully acknowledging the risks and by shaping a new culture where caring for employees is still an important value, but where performance is the measure and the source of reward.

STEPPING UP

When a company goes through 10 years of steady downsizing and finds itself still fighting to survive, fear and negativity are potent forces and can act as a brake against initiatives for renewal. Add to this situation a predictable strain in relationships between workers and management, and you have a work climate not particularly conducive for organizational learning. In this section, we'll visit a company that stepped up to such a challenge, and is continuing to learn how to turn adversity to advantage.

CASE PROFILE

GS TECHNOLOGIES

When GS Technologies took over Armco Worldwide Grinding Systems in Kansas City, it was acquiring a long tradition in steel making. The Kansas City Works had made steel for over a hundred years, first as the Kansas City Bolt & Nut Company in 1888. As recently as the early 1980s, it had employed over 5,000 people.

But since the 1970s, the American steel industry has been in steep decline. GST saw 60 percent of its capacity eliminated and three quarters of its product lines shut down. The Kansas City plant had been transformed from an old-line steel mill, making hundreds of products, to a specialized manufacturer with two main product lines.

GST also saw its workforce dwindle to about 1,000 people. Those who had survived the layoffs felt none too secure about their own jobs or about GST's future. As Rob Cushman, GST's president, admitted, "I think our workers felt like there was nothing they could do to save our company."[3] Nor did managers have the answers. Looking back, B. C. Huselton III, GS Technologies' vice president of Human and Business Systems, remarked,

> The largest difficulty we had was in even admitting we had a problem. We were in decline. . . . And I think our way to get around actually talking about it was to manage by denying it. It was clear to everybody that if we didn't make a major adjustment in the way we delivered our products, in the way we created new technology within our markets, and the way we behaved as an organization with each other, and with our customers, we weren't going to be around.[4]

GST did take some important steps towards rebuilding with its product line changes and the introduction of new technologies.

But there still remained the problem of rallying a shell-shocked workforce around a new, future orientation requiring their full commitment and support. For starters, this task involved dealing with some predictably strained labor–management relationships. While the company was selling off businesses and laying off workers, union leaders had become understandably cynical about management's plans for the future of the plant.

Building a Future

The strategy that GST management and Local 13 of the United Steelworkers of America worked up together was aptly called TeamWorks. It had its inspiration from a visit that union president John Cottrell made to a Delco-Remy automotive components plant in Anderson, Indiana. Delco-Remy had also experienced declining productivity and suffered too from poor relations between labor and management.

But Delco-Remy was able to turn its situation around with a highly successful employee team initiative that generated significant gains in efficiency and quality. Union members and managers had worked closely together to organize and implement the program, which yielded huge cost savings for the company. The program had also produced a much improved work climate, with enhanced morale and a greater spirit of cooperation.

The visit convinced Cottrell to attempt a similar venture at GS Technologies. His first task was to secure the cooperation of GST president Rob Cushman. Previous employee participation efforts had, as a rule, been designed and initiated solely by management, and had not been very successful. But Cushman agreed to work with Cottrell.

By building the program together, Cushman and Cottrell were already setting a precedent. Cottrell's second challenge was to sell his membership on the idea. Despite strong doubts about the company's seriousness in inviting workers to team up for such an initiative, a divided membership voted to give it a try.

Launching TeamWorks

Phase I of TeamWorks sought to build awareness and support for the undertaking. A voluntary process, TeamWorks required broad participation from a workforce that had rarely been asked to think or act for the company, beyond the basic requirements of their jobs. An innovative communications campaign was launched that focused on GS Technologies' plant employees. The campaign was informed by a series of focus groups, conducted at every level of the organization. The focus groups aimed to raise employee issues, as well as concerns and aspirations for GST's future.

There were several parts to this communications effort. Five hundred and thirty employees signed and returned "commitment cards," pledging their support to reorienting the company. GST and Local 13 took an ad in the *Kansas City Star*. It featured 500 employee signatures under a statement of renewed pride and purpose at GST. But the most well-received component of the campaign was probably a company calendar that featured brief stories about achievements of GST employees, and was mailed to everyone. The stories were submitted by fellow employees. Over 600 nominations were turned in.

Stories tended to focus on individuals, but some hailed the accomplishments of teams. All had the effect of a congratulatory message. In saluting a variety of success stories, the company was also introducing employees to each other as *achievers*. The intent of each page of the calendar was in fact to portray employees as the achievers they were and could continue to be. Each month featured a different subject. Next to the text appeared a photo. Here's one example: an account about a steelworker, submitted by a family member who also worked in the plant.

> He has been at GS Technologies going on 23 years. He has been married for 27. He hasn't had a beer for five months. He used to drink all the time. His family is very proud of him. So are the guys at work. Everyone can see a big change in him.

TeamWorks at Work

The most visible changes produced by TeamWorks came about through Phase II. Phase II was an all-employee program that asked seven-member employee teams to suggest ways to reduce costs, build revenue, or enhance the quality of worklife. The intent was to give all employees, at all levels, an equal voice in developing ideas that would make the company more productive, more profitable, and more fulfilling for its workers.

The program required that each team include at least one manager and one union member. Ideas submitted by the teams were reviewed by evaluation committees that also contained at least one manager and one union member. When an idea was accepted, points toward merchandise awards, valued at about a quarter of the idea's annualized net worth, were shared among team members. To be accepted, an idea needed to be accompanied by a cost justification and an implementation plan.

As one union member noted, "Probably, the man on the job knows best how to set up procedures to do his job. Where it used to be, you had a boss, he told you to do it, you went and did it—right, wrong, or indifferent. But now, somebody's listening." TeamWorks was all about listening. It assumed that every employee was worth listening to, and it encouraged people to come up with new thinking and new ideas.

Against a history of distrust and hostility, GS Technologies was staging an exercise in organizational learning that relied on cooperation and joint problem solving. Seventy percent of the eligible employee base enrolled in the program, fielding 80 active teams. Nearly 500 cost reduction or revenue generating ideas and over 500 ideas for improving work processes and job satisfaction were submitted. Forty-six percent of those ideas were approved, representing over $5 million of documented savings. Employee grievances also decreased, by about 40 percent. As Rob Cushman observed, "We're seeing things happening here that are not happening anywhere else in the steel industry."[5]

One particular idea didn't save the company any money, but symbolized the gains made in labor-management cooperation. The idea involved moving a 27-foot-tall, rope-driven flywheel from one of the plant's former turn-of-the-century mills. The flywheel would then be erected near the highway leading to the GS Technologies plant, as a monument to the workers who labored in the mill. Volunteers from management and union will see to its implementation.

SAFETY IN NUMBERS

The managers and workers of GS Technologies stepped forward together to reshape their company. They collaborated from the outset to design a process for learning and knowledge building. They invested in communicating their intentions, as well as the new directions they wanted to move in. They followed through with problem-solving teams to improve operating practices. Cost savings generated from the team activities were shared with teams, thereby rewarding and reinforcing the habits of continuous learning and innovation.

GS Technologies accomplished some significant organizational learning. It did so first by creating the conditions where people could be listened to and heard and where they could speak out without fear. Edgar Schein's *pre*scription for managing organizational learning and transformation provides a good *de*scription of what GST actually did.

> The problem . . . is to overcome the negative effects of past carrots and sticks, especially past sticks. To make people feel safe in learning, they must have motive, a sense of direction, and the opportunity to try out new things without fear of punishment. Sticks are not very useful during the learning process. Once the learning is underway, the carrot is the essential learning tool.[6]

The GS Technologies experience as well as the similar experience of Delco-Remy were successful in enlisting large numbers of employees to serve as positive critics of the status quo. At the same time, these employees created alternatives that represented measurable gains in quality and productivity for their companies. The key strategy for prompting participation and risk taking was teams.

Team activity has several attributes that encourage the kind of effort seen here and in several other case profiles presented earlier. Chief among them are that teams reinforce:

- the social appropriateness of learning and contributing to knowledge, as well as
- the confidence of individuals to challenge old understandings.

Katzenbach and Smith make this observation about the power of teams to make organizational learning happen:

> Behavioral change also occurs more readily in the team context. Because of their collective commitment, teams are not as threatened by change as are individuals left to fend for themselves. . . . Finally, because of their focus on performance, teams motivate, challenge, reward, and support individuals who are trying to change the way they do things.[7]

As a source of motivation, challenge, reward, and support, teams can be instrumental in facilitating organizational learning. We'll revisit the subject of teams and their impact on learning in each of the remaining chapters.

Chapter Ten

Sharing Control at Cadillac

The manager's task is no longer one of ensuring conformity and control; the over-riding challenge now becomes one of fostering a strong and constructive level of debate.

Matthew Kiernan[1]

Companies that maintain tight controls over access to information are placing limits on the uses that can be made from that information. In so doing, they are also limiting their potential to learn and to build knowledge. Companies that restrict participation in decision making and strategy building are tying up their organization's intellectual assets and reaping minimal return from the minds of their people.

The American automotive industry, from manufacturing to retailing, has been cited in the past for failing to share and use information and for maintaining highly bureaucratic, top down controls over its operations. Relationships within corporate, as well as within dealerships, and finally, between corporate and its dealer body, have not always supported organizational learning with its needs for openness and a "constructive level of debate."

GM'S STANDARDS

In the late 1980s, most American automotives were actively addressing not only the quality of their products, but also the quality of their customer service. GM leadership determined that it would revisit—through surveys, focus groups, and various work committees—what its present clientele expected and valued in the way of service relationships. GM actually targeted two sets of expectations. One was the expectations that car buyers and car owners had in their dealings with GM and its retail partners. The other was the expectations held by retailers regarding their relationship with the company's wholesale arm.

Once a clearer picture of customer expectations was established, GM moved to translate expectations into a new set of performance standards. Obtaining a consensus involved much give and take among GM dealers, GM service parts operations, and wholesale representatives from GM's marketing divisions. In the end, GM and its dealers came up with a set of standards that promised quality and consistency in dealing with customers. What also emerged was a customer-driven plan of action for continuous improvement, at both the retail and wholesale levels.

John Smith, GM's CEO, spoke candidly about the need for standards and about the importance of walking the talk:

> We're working hard to make the entire organization customer-driven in every sense of the term. There are many dealers who can easily think of examples of how arrogance and myopia extended in our relations. . . . Deeds, not words: that's the way we intend to run the business.[2]

CORRECTING MYOPIA AND ARROGANCE AT CADILLAC

Since the entry of the Japanese nameplates, the luxury car market has changed considerably. "To be honest," admits Jeff Pritchard, manager for Dealer Programs at Cadillac, "in 1990 we were beaten to the punch by Lexus. Lexus put together the ultimate customer experience. They set the standard." Pritchard added that there was some irony here in that "Lexus was hiring Cadillac people and people from other American car companies. And they were grabbing our dealers too."

At the time, Pritchard was in Cadillac's Service Division. He had already begun to think that the ideas of Deming and the notion of service as a process were keys to strengthening Cadillac's competitive position. One of the moving forces for Pritchard and other Cadillac people was a Cadillac dealer named Carl Sewell. As Pritchard describes him, "He was ahead of his time in a lot of areas. He had listened to Crosby, and he was familiar with Deming before we had gotten into it. His constant challenge to us was 'Cadillac needs to be my teacher: where do I go to learn how to be the best service organization in the world? You guys ought to bring that to me, and you don't.'"

Pritchard and several others responded to this challenge by first creating a kind of "skunk works" for service improvement. Out of this activity came a proposal to study service as a process, so that when a dealer asked for help in improving customer service, Cadillac's Service Division would have a model from which to offer reliable and consistent advice. Process modeling, borrowing heavily on Deming and the quality gurus, became the strategy. And a logical outcome would be a set of performance standards.

To make the skunk works more legitimate, Cadillac created the position of Manager of Dealer Service Process. Jeff Pritchard was its first occupant. "The whole idea," he explained, "was that we had to look at service not as a piecemeal, happenstance experience that was put together from a bunch of separate pieces—and that if you were lucky came together in a good, satisfying experience. We had to look at it as a *process*."

"Actually," he continued, "the service process is very intricate. There are a lot of things going on at the same time. It is more than just fixing the car. It's more than just a system to wait on the customer. We had to understand all the things that go into the total service experience. And one of the things we wanted to understand more about was the idea of customer *expectations* versus customer *experiences*. We had traditionally measured customers' experiences, but we never really got at what their expectations were."

Meeting Expectations

Greg Warner is Cadillac's director of Service Administration. Looking back at Pritchard's study of dealer service practices, he commented, "Jeff had a mission to look at the service side of our business, kind of grab it by its throat, shake it up a little bit, and start all over again. The idea was to put something together that met *everybody's* expectations—ours, our customers, our dealers—and involved a fresh look at how we did business with one another.

"It was about this time that the sales organization also became interested in making some changes. New people in new positions saw a need to cooperate more closely with service. We began pooling resources around initiatives that developed awareness of customer expectations, and which increased the level of professionalism that Cadillac and its dealers brought to serving their customers. There was less proprietary thinking, more 'We're going to have to cooperate and graduate.'"

Warner also noted that there was a conscious decision almost from the outset to work closely with the dealers. "We've probably always wrongly given more emphasis to the retail side of our business. We started off talking more about the retail organization, but quickly turned around, because the dealers reminded us pretty early on that, 'Hey guys, if you're going to hold us to all these standards, you have to get into the same process yourselves. We expect certain things of *you*, and you're going to have to operate to certain standards too.' I guess also that it was crucial for dealers to see that if Cadillac wanted them to go the extra mile and do a lot of extra things, then Cadillac would have to step up and do something extra as well."

"Together," continued Warner, "we needed to build a process that would make the customer experience a more satisfactory one. The fact that GM had committed to identifying a common set of standards made our idea a lot easier to get implemented. GM managers across divisions and disciplines joined to develop these standards. And we're talking about the whole ownership cycle, not just the buying experience."

Targeted Customer Research

To begin to answer these questions for their own customers, Cadillac commissioned a massive research project, bringing together groups of customers and groups of employees around the issue of customer expectations. Over several months, more than 700 focus groups were conducted. As Greg Warner explained, "We needed to have specific information about each dealership. This is not a one-size-fits-all situation. You've got to research each dealer's customers. And I can tell you, the focus groups got people's attention. They really got us thinking about what was on customers' minds."

Warner noted a major shift in the GM survey procedure. "We're going to change our CSi (customer satisfaction index). We won't do the six month survey like we've been doing for 15 years. We'll switch to two different surveys, one shortly after the delivery, which will measure how we met their expectations in the sale and delivery process—based on the GM standards. In the other, we'll begin to survey our customers after they have a warranty return. And that means whether the car is four months old or approaching four years old. If it's covered by warranty, we will survey those customers and ask them again, based on standards, 'How well are we doing?'"

Because of GM's new research plans, Warner added, "Cadillac can kind of change its focus a little bit. We can branch out and look at some issues that are important to *us*. Right now, we're doing nothing but talking with people we've managed to sell a car to. That's great: those are the people we want to take care of. But maybe we want to focus a little bit more on people that we *didn't* sell a car to. Why didn't they see fit to do business with us? What might we have done to them in the service area that drove them away from us?"

Jeff Pritchard acknowledged that Cadillac indeed had a need to learn from noncustomers. "You know," he began, "we have product plans that we hope are going to attract a customer that we've never seen before. Somewhere along the way, we need to learn about those people, their expectations, and whether they differ from our traditional folks."

STANDARDS FOR EXCELLENCE: THE CADILLAC OF PERFORMANCE IMPROVEMENT

Cadillac has already recognized that a new clientele comes equipped with some different expectations. They're a younger, more sophisticated kind of car buyer who is also inclined to be more critical of the sales and service experience. Partly as a response to this demand for higher levels of customer service, but more as the logical follow-through from the work on *service as a process*, Cadillac designed with its dealers a continuous improvement process that would involve both retail and wholesale participation.

Called Standards for Excellence, the process aims to engage dealership personnel and Cadillac staff in a systematic effort to improve customer satisfaction. The focus is on the entire buying and ownership experience. It is perhaps the automotive industry's most comprehensive performance improvement initiative.

The effort is guided by the GM standards. It relies on store-based customer research to tee up improvement projects. Projects are shaped and implemented by employee teams in each participating dealership. At regular intervals, dealership performance is evaluated according to key performance indicators. Achievement of performance goals leads to gain-sharing and recognition awards.

Cadillac's Standards for Excellence is built upon the concept of sharing information and control for performance improvement. It is organized around the following five components.

1. **Dealer-based customer research.** For each enrolled dealer, GM's marketing research partner conducts surveys and focus groups with that dealer's customers and, separately, with the dealership's employees. The research is designed to identify areas that need improvement and gaps that exist between customer expectations and what employees think customers expect and between expected levels of service delivery and actual performance.

2. **Facilitated planning.** With a Cadillac zone representative in attendance, a trained facilitator presents research findings to each dealership's leadership team. The leadership team typically comprises the dealer principal, the general manager, and managers of parts, service, finance and insurance, and sales. This cross-functional management group works together to identify the dealership's best opportunities for improvement, then targets the areas they want to work on first.

3. **Continuous improvement teams.** The facilitators next coach cross-functional teams of dealership employees to

develop action plans for closing customer satisfaction gaps. Teams hold regular meetings over the year to develop and implement solutions to problems and to create customer service enhancements. The outcomes are either revised work processes or improvements in execution. New teams are formed to address new targets identified by the research and by the leadership team.

4. **Performance measurement.** Dealers are measured quarterly against a comprehensive set of operating criteria tied to the standards. Criteria include customer satisfaction ratings (CSI), sales effectiveness, sales and service professionalism, parts management, and completion of sales and technical training programs. A variety of measurement methods are used, including customer surveys, "mystery shoppers" (researchers posing as car buyers), and tabulation of sales results.

5. **Rewards and recognition.** At year-end, top scoring dealer-management teams earn travel and education awards. In addition, dealers can earn cash bonuses when certain CSI and incremental sales performance goals are met.

SORTING IT OUT

Mark LaNeve is Cadillac's Director of Advertising and Marketing Planning. As he reflected on the progress of Standards for Excellence, he held onto a big cigar, which went unsmoked. He said he's stopped smoking. This is his "pacifier."

"Cadillac's always had a good dealer body," LaNeve observed, "and I think everybody basically believes that satisfying customers is important. But now I think the dealers are learning that customer satisfaction is really good business. Once the right processes are in place, everything in the dealership runs better."

LaNeve had been especially impressed by the effect of the dealer-based research. "I think, first of all, that the research surprised them. It was a significant emotional event to see their own customers in focus groups. A dealership is a classical example of a hierarchical organization. There's one guy who's the boss, and he generally owns the place. And like with any boss, you're not going to feed him bad news all day long if you can avoid it. So I think in some cases dealers were shocked to see that there were gaps in delivering to customers' expectations. I think they learned from it because they probably thought they had been doing a real good job."

"The classic example," LaNeve continued, "was dealers who had free service loaners. OK, they've got free service loaners, and they think the customers are happy. But a lot of customers said they weren't happy because some dealerships wouldn't *offer* the loaner to them. They had to ask, and it was embarrassing for them to go and say, 'Can I have a loaner?' "

Store-specific research, with customers providing detailed, anecdotal feedback, created many new insights for dealers. "Before," LaNeve observed, "when we only had the CSi, the dealer could look at the scores and see he had a problem with delivery. But he didn't know how important the problem was to his customers, and he didn't know what was actually wrong about delivery."

LEADERSHIP TEAMS: SHARING INFORMATION AT THE TOP

LaNeve noticed another change in dealer management behavior that held promise for continuous learning gains. "Traditionally," he remarked, "every person in a dealership works pretty independently. That's just the nature of the beast. You wouldn't see a lot of meetings going on in dealerships. I'm not saying they *should* be having a lot of meetings. But many of the problems we're facing are there because service and sales weren't talking together to get the car prepped and delivered to the customer right. Or new cars and used cars weren't working together, or parts wasn't working closely with the service department.

"What would happen is that you'd find out you had a problem with delivery, and the sales manager would say, 'It's those guys in service. They don't know what they're doing.' And the service manager would say, 'Well, the sales guys promised the car to the customer way before we could get it ready.' It was like rocks being thrown over a wall.

"Now, I think we're moving to an environment where the managers are working more in teams. It's a more horizontal organization. When the leadership teams get their research findings and they know they have a problem with new car delivery, they bring representatives from parts, service, new car prep, and sales together in a room and ask, 'What's the best way to solve this problem?' Now we hear them saying, 'It's a problem we have in common, so let's find a solution together.'"

LaNeve saw Cadillac's primary role here to "work with dealers and their managers to foster that kind of environment. Dealers aren't resistant to it," he acknowledged. "It's just different."

SHARING INFORMATION WITH EMPLOYEE TEAMS

The other big difference brought about by Standards for Excellence is the role in process improvement being played by employee teams. Kurt McNeil, who took over the job of Dealer Service Process Manager from Jeff Pritchard, sees this development as a rather natural one. "With the standards, we have a structure from which to start looking at the pieces of the process—how customers are handled at different places in sales and service. If you're going to start breaking down a process and really look at how you're currently doing something, your frontline people are the ones who are going to have to identify the process and the opportunities for improvement.

"They're the ones who know. The dealer doesn't know. The managers don't know. It's the frontline people who are dealing with it on a daily basis. You have to tap into them, and the way to tap into them is with *teams.*"

McNeil saw the teams as having only begun to hit their stride. "By involving the frontline employees, you can come up with little process improvements, like parking the cars in the right place, and making sure the technicians turn the keys into the cashier, and not telling all the customers to pick up their car at five o'clock. But then they can take it a step further. As teams develop their ideas, we're working with them on how to do cost-benefit analysis."

Learning about Learning

Greg Warner observed that the team problem-solving experience was challenging the ways in which dealers regarded the whole issue of process improvement. "With some of these ideas from the teams, you'll hear comments like, 'You should have thought about that a long time ago!' Well, the fact of the matter is that retail operations are pretty chaotic. In most cases, it's the crisis of the moment. It's 'let's get through the day.' It's 'handle this problem, take care of that irate customer.' So this is almost the first opportunity for a lot of them to ever sit down and take a few moments to think about what they do. It's the first time they can stop and say, 'You know, if we did it a little bit different, it might have a big impact on customer satisfaction.'"

If the dealers had been surprised by some of the research findings, they were probably even more surprised by the level of participation in these team activities. In most cases, dealerships saw over 50 percent of the staff volunteering to participate *immediately* after the initial meeting introducing the team concept. That percentage has grown steadily since.

Warner observed that "the reaction of the employees was beyond anybody's expectation. The dealers, I think, were shocked to see how their employees responded to the opportunity to get involved and have an impact on how things are done." As Kurt McNeil concluded, "They want to contribute. They want to have a say in what happens in the dealership."

Facilitating Continuous Improvement

The Cadillac team agrees that the Standards for Excellence facilitators have been a key factor in the success of the continuous improvement team process.

"We knew," explained McNeil, "that we couldn't just put together a set of books, send them out to the dealers, and say 'Here, do these things and you're going to be in good shape.'"

Working with about 15 dealers apiece, the facilitators first served as process catalysts. They helped get things started, and they've helped keep things going. As Jeff Pritchard noted, "Without the facilitators, Standards for Excellence would have been dead on arrival." At Cadillac, the facilitators are agents for information sharing, for group problem solving, and for cooperative learning.

CONTINUOUS LEARNING ACROSS THE ORGANIZATION

The Cadillac team has learned a lot about process improvement, but they're also learning about how to support continuous learning across the organization.

"In my opinion," said Kurt McNeil, "you have to have all of the components. You have to have the research, which gives you the detail and the awareness. You have to train: You have to give them the 'how'—you can't just give them the 'what.' You have to have the appropriate types of measures because you're asking them to steer by what's important. And you have to have some kind of rewards or recognition, at least a process, that reaches out and addresses what's important."

McNeil also made the point that while learning is taking place at the dealership level, it's also affecting the larger organization. "We've concentrated the research on each specific dealer. But this information gives us a national composite, so we can be looking at the big things that need to be worked on—and improved upon—and so we can distribute our resources accordingly."

Cadillac dealers have made good use of Standards for Excellence. Dealers pay from $10,000 to $15,000 each to participate. Practically all of the top dealers (375, who account for approximately 74 percent of retail volume) are enrolled. CSi ratings are up significantly since the inception of the program, and the progress in CSi for enrolled dealers has outpaced that for dealers who are not enrolled.

For Greg Warner, Standards for Excellence is a process itself, with a built-in capacity to renew itself. He remarked that with the quarterly cycle of measurement, feedback, and recognition, each new quarter is "like a whole new ball game. They start out again, and it gives them another opportunity to achieve. They're all interested in treating the customer well. This just keeps the interest level there."

Kurt McNeil sees Standards for Excellence putting new value on learning as the key element of a continuous improvement culture. "It's all a part of the message that we send to the dealers—that what's really important is that they're learning something, that they're making changes, and that they're seeing positive improvement."

CONSTRUCTIVE DEBATE

Cadillac has embarked on a process of constructive internal debate. It involves dialog between the organization and its customers and between wholesale and retail. It involves departmental managers in the dealership, as well as cross-functional teams within dealerships.

The process aims to improve customer service and the operating routines that contribute to serving the customer. It is also a process that can create its own tensions as individuals question the status quo and argue alternative points of view. James Kiernan has called these tensions the inevitable product of "constructive contention," which in turn must be regarded as a potential source of "organizational dynamism and renewal":

> Constructive contention is directly related to organizational learning: it requires a willingness, even an eagerness to continually reexamine critically those assumptions and orthodoxies which deaden a company's environmental scanning equipment and inhibit lateral thinking and creativity.[3]

Cadillac *and* its dealers are learning and changing because they're convinced it's in their best interests to do so. Their initiative to extend to everyone in the organization the responsibility and the resources (in particular, information and training) to contribute to performance improvement is paying off. Against an industry tradition of strong bureaucratic control, Cadillac and its retail partners are providing an instructive demonstration of that under-realized concept, *empowerment.*

Chapter Eleven

Prompting Change at American Airlines

We must become able not only to transform our institutions, in response to changing situations and requirements; we must invent and develop institutions which are "learning systems," that is to say, systems capable of bringing about their own continuing transformation.

Donald Schön[1]

In a business world where technology and market forces never stand still, a company that is not positioned to keep pace with or to lead change risks falling behind. Unfortunately, it's a rather natural tendency to want to stand pat, especially for companies that are established and successful. Peter Drucker sees this tendency as a significant barrier that all established organizations need to surmount.

> Society, community, family are all conserving institutions. They try to maintain stability and to prevent, or at least slow down, change. But the organization of the postcapitalist society of organizations is a destabilizer. Because its function is to put knowledge to work—on tools, processes, and products; on work; on knowledge itself—it must be organized for constant change. It must be organized for innovation.[2]

For companies that occupy positions of leadership in their industries, it is not easy to think of working to *destabilize* the organization. Neither is it easy to invite individuals who have worked to shape their own personal areas of success to act in ways that might compromise them. The type of organization that Drucker is calling for must somehow counteract the forces of conservation, at least to the extent that learning and knowledge building can continue to facilitate *advantageous change.*

One destabilizing strategy is to create simulations where managers are challenged to test their fundamental assumptions against different and unfamiliar scenarios. As administered by various management consultants and executive education programs, these exercises require participants to rethink the adequacy of their assumptions and beliefs and to generate alternative solutions as necessary. A dramatic example of this kind of management learning exercise is one designed by military strategist Andrew Marshall, described below.

> A classified war game at the U.S. Naval War College recently pitted a militarily resurgent China in the year 2020 against the U.S. The U.S. was badly bloodied—despite the best efforts of the 80 participating military officers, intelligence analysts, and Defense Department strategists.
>
> The key difference between the hypothetical adversaries was that China had a 21st-century military, bought off the shelf, while the U.S. fielded an updated version of its Gulf War force. . . . [The game was] about whether the way wars are fought will change fundamentally in coming decades.[3]

This game's key ingredient was a plausible future situation, designed to expose how conventional approaches to cope with a problem would lead to failure. Since failure in a war game leads to disaster, the message comes across with some punch. Presumably, the game also led to the formulation of some alternative tactics, based upon a revised set of assumptions about how to wage war after the rules of the game have changed.

ADVANCING SUCCESS WITH TEAMS

Another strategy for counteracting the complacency and inertia that success can bring is a continuous learning initiative involving everyone in the organization. Founded upon self-questioning and aimed at revitalizing work processes, this form of organizational learning can be a powerful force for renewal and change. As applied by industry leaders like American Airlines and Ford Motor Company, the strategy finds a special energy in the deployment of continuous learning teams.

INNOVAATIONS

American Airlines is the largest commercial airline company in the world. In a deregulated and highly competitive industry, American continues to look for ways to add value to its product and to bring its product to market in the most profitable way. In 1986, American launched a major organizational learning initiative that continues to this day. Its goals were then, as they are now, twofold: to improve the balance sheet and to involve employees throughout the organization in enhancing performance in every dimension of airline operations.

American had run suggestion programs in the past, so when it announced another program, this time to encourage team-developed ideas with documented profit impact, employees greeted it with skepticism. Most employees perceived that the company would maintain a low level of commitment to soliciting and acting upon new ideas. Their opinion, however, has changed.

InnovAAtions (chronically misspelled) looked different from the beginning. Teams could earn significant merchandise awards for approved ideas. And ideas were evaluated with minimal delay. With a strong communications campaign and solid backing from Bob Crandall, the CEO, *InnovAAtions* took off with 3,428 teams from across the company. In less than four months, the program had produced 1,660 adopted ideas, yielding in excess of $53 million in first year net savings or revenue.

Institutionalizing Innovation

The success of this venture led American to make plans for a permanent company-wide idea generation process. Modeled on the strengths of the pilot, the plans carried the promise of continued top management leadership and support. Bob Stoltz, the coordinator of *InnovAAtions*, assumed responsibility over a staff of seven full-time idea analysts, chosen from finance, engineering, and industrial engineering, to handle suggestion analysis. American called the process *IdeAAs in Action*. Employees from all facets of the airline's headquarters, operations, reservations, and sales divisions, were invited to participate.

Looking back at seven years of continuous *IdeAAs in Action* activity, Stoltz feels a sense of accomplishment in the progress they've made. Now operating with a staff of 85 to administer idea submission, evaluation, and implementation, Stoltz remarked, "We've become a part of the culture." *IdeAAs* has indeed produced some remarkable statistics:

- Over $350 million in audited, bottom-line profit contribution.
- 20 percent annual participation (from 12,000 employees).
- 150-200 ideas submitted per day.
- 25 percent of all ideas approved.

Three work forces in particular contribute to these numbers. Airplane maintenance enjoys almost 50 percent participation each year, generating 60 percent of the net savings. They tend to focus on preventing parts from breaking or wearing down, repairing broken parts, or identifying alternate vendors that can provide better, more cost-beneficial services. Reservations and ticketing concentrate on making procedures more efficient and responsive to customer needs.

Tracking Results

"What separates American's program from others," explains Stoltz, "is the way we track and evaluate the process. We don't try to approve ideas just for the sake of approving them. We make an effort to qualify and measure ideas. There are a lot of checks and balances in the system. The program is audited each year by our internal auditing team, and they've concluded that it's producing a return to the company that's actually greater than we're aware of when we approve the ideas."

Two other features of the tracking system bear mention. First, every idea valued over $50,000 is audited during year two to corroborate savings—and possibly to increase payout to the submitting team. The other feature is the "150 Day Report." If the responsible department manager has not responded to an employee idea within 150 days, it is given to Bob Crandall for review. As Bob Stoltz pointed out, "Many ideas that are slow to get resolved get decided on by the 149th day." He added that another impact of the program is that managers are now more likely to reach decisions, and not delay.

Demonstrating seriousness and concern for ideas through prompt response to the suggestor has long been a key factor in achieving employee satisfaction with a suggestion program. It is not surprising that American's process scores a healthy "76 percent effective" rating among employees, who are queried regularly as part of a comprehensive employee opinion survey.

Celebrating accomplishments is also a core component in keeping the process top-of-mind for employees. Annual leadership receptions and dinners are held, hosted by Crandall and other senior officers of American. *IdeAAs* is also reported on at each of the annual President's Conferences held in major hub cities around the country.

Several years ago, American engaged in its most conspicuous celebration related to *IdeAAs*. "We wanted to come up with something that would show our people and our stockholders that our program was important," Stoltz recalled. "So we tried to think of something tangible we could do with the profits we had generated. We decided to buy an airplane—a $50 million twin engine Boeing 757." Sometime afterwards, CEO Crandall led 200 American employees to Seattle for the maiden voyage of "The Pride of American."

Hurdles

The leading drags against higher idea generation and implementation are typically two barriers of perception. Stoltz still encounters a bias—most frequently with engineers—against "paying people for their ideas" (That's their job!). He also encounters from time to time the fear that an idea, once implemented, will embarrass someone. "If it wasn't invented by me, I'm probably not doing my job right" is the alleged implication. Stoltz points out that American has pioneered the strategy of rewarding idea implementers, recognizing them for instituting change. "Every time you change," concedes Stoltz, "you're at risk. Over the years, that fear has decreased. But it's still out there. That's human nature."

Stoltz tells the story of how the financial department once took issue with what seemed to them to be an unreasonable level of award earmarked for a particular implementer, a departmental manager in maintainance. Senior management was asked to review the matter. As part of their review, they took note of the fact that the maintenance manager was well-regarded and that his group had the best attendance records and the lowest amount of overtime in the department. The man's department had also implemented over 300 ideas, producing more than $19 million in savings.

Stolz remembers Bob Crandall summing up senior management's verdict with the comment, "Maybe we should have more departmental managers like him." And there's an ironic twist to the story. The maintenance department manager has since been promoted to a managing director position. But it's a level where he is no longer eligible to earn awards as an implementer.

Sustaining Participation

According to Stoltz, American has developed, over the life of the program, a healthy appreciation for the power of team innovation. "Researching our areas of strength in recent years and analyzing those results, it was apparent that we needed to spotlight team formation. Eleven percent of our ideas were from teams but they produced 50 percent of the total value.

"We're looking for the right balance between getting participation and ideas and getting ideas with impact," Stoltz added. One of the keys to maintaining participation levels is keeping people in the game, especially after they've submitted an idea and and are notified that it's not approved. "People sometimes underestimate the power of ownership of these ideas," explained Stoltz. "When you turn them down, it can be like telling them that their baby is ugly.

"We give a detailed response to an idea, even if we're turning it down because it's a duplicate idea. And we get a lot of duplicate ideas." To insure that submitters can get a full hearing, the program has also created an appeals board. Any suggestors who are still not satisfied that their idea has been understood and given a fair reading can get another review there.

"This year," he continued, "we're launching a new campaign called *IdeAAs at Home*. We're asking local managers to approve ideas themselves, rather than submitting them all to headquarters. We're empowering these managers to think for the company's best interests and to make decisions they can live with."

A Culture for Learning

American will continue to look to its employees to reinvent the way it does business. "We've developed the most cost-conscious culture in the airline industry," says Stoltz. "Our program has had an impact on people's thinking about how to deal with problems. Before, you might have known we were wasting money, but you didn't know where to take your ideas. Now you know."

Last year, more than $60 million dollars worth of employee knowledge building went to American's bottom line. "Idea generation," concludes Stoltz, "has become our competitive advantage."

Chapter Twelve

Prompting Change at Ford

[T]he common good is the pursuit of the good in common.

Dennis McCann[1]

At the beginning of the 1990s, Ford was enjoying considerable success. It had been the leader in the resurgence of the American automotive industry during the 80s. It was financially healthy and competitively strong. In 1992, the Ford Taurus was the top selling car in the U.S. "Quality Is Job 1" had become more than a winning slogan, and Ford sales had climbed as consumers saw product quality improve.

Ford's vision for continuing this improved performance was to find ways to strengthen *continuous improvement* as a business strategy. In particular, they saw tapping into the creative and intellectual power of their employees—*all* their employees—as a key element in this business strategy. One of the most obvious vehicles for channeling employee ideas for improvement was their employee suggestion system.

RUNNING ON EMPTY

Ford has had a suggestion program in place since 1947. In its day, it was one of the best employee involvement processes in American industry. The Japanese came over to study it, and in 1951, Toyota had borrowed from it. Unlike the Japanese, however, Ford did not concentrate on improving the process over time, and it had remained pretty much the same operation for some 40 years.

By 1990, the Ford suggestion system was a tired, underperforming machine. Few suggestions were submitted—less than .1 per employee per year. Only 7 percent of the workforce participated, which was slightly below the U.S. average of 9 percent. Salaried employees were not allowed to submit ideas relating to their own jobs. There were long delays in the idea evaluation process, which over the years had come to discourage idea submission.

Ford understood that Japanese auto manufacturers had a significant competitive advantage because they were better at listening to, and learning from, their employees. In July 1991, Ford convened a 15-member Suggestion Program Reevaluation Committee to consider what might be done to revive this aspect of continuous improvement. Part of the committee's task was to analyze its own programs, both domestic and international. But the committee also benchmarked a number of different firms, including Japanese companies.

Ford came away with the impression that the Japanese suggestion processes were among the most critical components of their continuous improvement efforts. Japanese product quality and process efficiency both seemed to benefit. One of the suggestion processes that most impressed the committee was Toyota's. Red Maynard, by then the committee's chairperson, acknowledged how fitting it was that 40 years later, Ford might seek to borrow something back.

FORD'S CONTINUOUS IMPROVEMENT RECOGNITION SYSTEM

By Fall of 1992, the committee had put together a plan that would be far reaching in scope and ambition. The plan called for the introduction of a Continuous Improvement Recognition System, or CIRS, for short. CIRS would be an operations-driven endeavor with performance goals and specific measurement criteria, to guide its progress. CIRS would eventually involve the entire company of over 325,000 employees and approximately 200 facilities located around the world.

CIRS Objectives

CIRS is an engine that drives organizational learning. It is designed to help Ford people generate and apply knowledge that will improve Ford products and operations. CIRS is deliberately named. It aims not only to stimulate thinking and learning, but also to capture that learning for *continuous improvement* purposes. It is a *system* in its approach to integrating communications, training, tracking, and rewards. And it uses *recognition* to make things happen. Here are the 10 objectives that the committee developed for CIRS.

CIRS Objectives

1. Encourage all employees to actively participate in improving the operations of Ford.
2. Develop employee skills to create and contribute improvements within Ford.
3. Develop management ability to coach and mentor employees.
4. Enable all managers to make decisions about their operations.
5. Acknowledge the value of *all* improvements: financial, operational, environmental; large or small.
6. Encourage and reinforce teamwork and collaboration among employees, departments, and larger organizational units.
7. Facilitate the exchange of healthy communication and foster the development of trust between employees and their managers.
8. Provide significant recognition and reward opportunities to all employees for demonstrating commitment to continuous improvement and for successfully contributing to improvement.
9. Measure changes in activity levels and organizational impact, producing actionable data to chart the future course of continuous improvement at Ford.
10. Produce substantial quality and cost improvements and a healthy return on investment.

Measuring CIRS

Ford has chosen five quantitative measures to use in evaluating CIRS and its progress:

1. The percentage of eligible employees participating.
2. The number of ideas submitted per employee.
3. The approval rate for submitted ideas.
4. The average time taken to reach an evaluation decision.
5. The annual *implemented* savings per employee.

In addition, Ford will be looking at the impact CIRS has on the company in several broader areas: return on investment, employee attitudes, and work environment.

HOW CIRS WORKS: A BLUEPRINT FOR ORGANIZATIONAL LEARNING

CIRS is designed in accordance with the 10 objectives listed above. And the design is evolving. A steering committee of senior Ford executives meets quarterly with the CIRS manager to review activity and progress toward objectives. The steering committee may also make revisions to the design in order to improve the process. The steering committee is responsible for maintaining consistency and fairness in four basic aspects of the CIRS process: participant and idea eligibility; idea approval authority; measurement; and reward levels.

Ford expects all of its divisions and facilities to participate in CIRS, but decisions about readiness to join are made more or less independently. When an organization is ready to adopt CIRS, it meets with representatives from the CIRS management team to tailor the design of the CIRS process to the business and culture of that organization. The management of each organization determines its own CIRS budget, which will be allocated to operations. Management also decides on how time for idea generation activities will be budgeted. As the CIRS manager put it, "There's a lot of autonomy at Ford plants and a tradition of doing things the best way *as they see it*. But CIRS demands a uniform process for two reasons: effective communications, and equity."

Participation and Reinforcement

Both hourly and salaried employees can volunteer to participate. CIRS invites participants to recommend job- or process-related ways to improve productivity, quality, safety, ergonomics, and customer satisfaction. Suggestions for specific cost improvements are also welcomed. Ideas can be submitted by individuals or by teams, and *can* be related to the job or work area of the idea originator. Originators are responsible for documenting their ideas, including appropriate cost analysis. Ideas are submitted on the same basic form companywide. "We're trying to make it simple," the CIRS manager said of the submission process. "We're trying to get away from complexity."

If an idea is approved for implementation, the originators receive "Ford Points" based on the value of their idea. Ford Points can be accumulated, and are redeemable either for merchandise, for Ford vehicles, or for travel awards. Ford opted not to emphasize cash as an award for several reasons. Noncash awards are easier to promote and have greater "trophy value." Cash awards are also more likely to be confused with compensation; Ford wanted to differentiate CIRS earnings from regular pay plans. Finally, Ford realized that specific awards could become goals that employees would try to achieve. One consequence of this kind of goal setting is that teams might stay active longer and generate multiple ideas.

Ford especially encourages participants to form cross-functional idea teams, since such teams tend to be more productive. Working through teams also contributes to the achievement of at least half of the CIRS objectives. Team members earn equally for approved ideas, and then again when ideas are implemented.

CIRS uses Ford Points as incentives in a variety of strategic ways. One strategy to spur participation and to build management ownership allows supervisors to earn Ford Points each quarter based on the levels of participation from their groups. Departments can also earn awards based upon the total number of Ford Points accumulated annually by their employees. Still other strategies attach to different CIRS process functions, and will be mentioned later. Looking back over the years when the Ford suggestion program tended to produce a rather negligible return, Red

Maynard explained the strategic use of awards this way: "If you want to change behavior, you put some rewards next to those behaviors."

Idea Evaluation

The evaluation of submitted ideas is a critical function in CIRS. Since most ideas involve adjustments to someone's budget, their impact is both operational and financial. Given the CIRS objective to enable managers to make decisions about *their* operations, Ford wants active participation from all levels of management.

Ideas that claim value to Ford of $500 or less can be approved by an appropriate supervisor. Ideas valued at more than $500 are handed over to a departmental committee for evaluation. Ford sees *timely* processing of ideas as critical to the success of CIRS. If participants know their ideas will get reasonably prompt attention, they'll be more likely to generate them and to keep generating them.

The problem has always been how to make consideration of ideas a sufficient priority to warrant the right level of attention. CIRS has a goal to accept or reject all ideas within 44 days. To give this goal some weight, CIRS awards Ford Points each quarter to department managers and their committee members for keeping their average turnaround at or below 30 days.

The other critical aspect of idea evaluation is the extent to which idea decisions can serve as useable feedback by the originators. Several things are at stake here. If an idea is not accepted, the decision can be communicated in ways that prompt either further development, if appropriate, or at least encouragement to try again. When nonacceptance decisions are communicated without much information, or without sharing reasons, the learning potential is diminished, and so is the likelihood of continued participation.

CIRS addresses this issue in several ways. Evaluators are prepared to maximize the learning potential in their communications to teams. Ford Points are used to reward management behaviors that support active, continued employee participation. And the entire CIRS process and support structure are designed to promote cooperation and the involvement of different perspectives in the development and implementation of ideas. CIRS promotes organizational learning by helping good ideas grow into larger conversations, involving different jobs, departments, and business functions.

Idea Implementation

Once an idea is approved, it still must be implemented. Implementation represents another potential slow-down, with financial consequences to the company. In many cases, an idea can be implemented by the individual or team that originated it. In others—particularly larger scale improvements that involve more than one department—implementation is both an opportunity to extend learning and a challenge to get things done.

CIRS again uses incentives to capture the full value of new knowledge contained in approved ideas. Ford Points are awarded to individuals or teams for timely implementation of ideas. "The reason we give points to implementers," said CIRS's manager, "is to help make implementation happen. If you can hasten the implementation by seven to eight weeks, you can typically pay for all the award points they earn." CIRS can engage idea "sponsors" to extend the idea beyond its original boundaries as well.

Management and Infrastructure

CIRS operates with a manager and four staff people. They are responsible for coordinating operations with Ford management and with Ford business priorities. They also maintain operational oversight and introduce and launch CIRS at different sites across the Ford organization. This latter task involves adjusting CIRS to the cultural and operational environment of each participating facility. The CIRS management team is supported by nearly 100 people from an outside partner, the Maritz Performance Improvement Company, who assist in promotion, administration, training, and award fulfillment.

Leadership

At a meeting of field and headquarters people involved in running CIRS, nametags were required. One nametag simply said "Red."

"Now that (former Chairman Harold) Red Poling has retired," Red Maynard explained, "I'm the only Red left at Ford."

The individual who served as CIRS's first manager is Red Maynard. Red gave both shape and flavor to CIRS. He helped "birth" it, and he steered it through its critical early stages. In 1995 Red Maynard retired from Ford, and is now a private consultant living in Bloomfield Hills, Michigan. The extended interview with Red that follows was conducted before his retirement. It is prefaced by a short profile, and is intended primarily to describe CIRS from his rather unique and instructive vantage point.

Born and raised in Eastern Kentucky, with a soft accent to prove it, Roosevelt "Red" Maynard was a factory machinist before he went to college, where he studied mechanical engineering and nuclear physics. Ford hired him right out of engineering school.

Red Maynard's 37-year career at Ford has been primarily in engineering, mostly as a manager. Over that career, working in manufacturing, reliability, product, and design, and development engineering, he's gotten to know a lot about how cars are made. Red has also been a student of how things get done in a manufacturing business. While at Ford, Red earned his MBA in economics and industrial psychology from the University of Michigan, studying with Rensis Likert. Red's self-description of his background is a history of schooling and learning.

Most of us hold onto a few particularly memorable pieces of learning, often from earlier, more impressionable points in our careers. One of Red's remembered nuggets, acquired from his first boss, was "If someone looks like he knows what he's doing, you let him do it. Otherwise, it's like standing in the middle of a free flowing stream; you can dam it up."

You can get a sense of how Red has used that advice as the manager of his own group and how it would come to influence CIRS from an anecdote shared by a former direct report (and captured several years ago in a book on new management models):

There are no restrictions on how we do our job or where we go to do it. We cross section and unit lines all the time. Each of us has his own garden to look after, but we don't hesitate to suggest improvements elsewhere or to stroll over and confer with somebody else's people. Territories would get in the way. We're managing company resources to achieve common objectives. This summer, Red was out of town for five straight weeks. Like a good string quartet, we just kept right on performing.[2]

I asked Red Maynard how he came to be involved with CIRS. His response started with a lead-in line I would hear several times during the course of the morning. "Let me tell you a little story," is how he began.

Interview with Red Maynard, Former CIRS Manager

"Back in '91, I was invited to meet with a group of about 15 people, called the Suggestion Program Reevaluation Committee, that was going to take a look at Ford's suggestion program. I had already started my own suggestion program in EMDO (Engine Manufacturing Development Operations), so they invited me to their meeting to talk about my program. Well, there was someone else from Ford who had run a program and myself and an outside company.

"We all spoke, and afterwards there was a push to have the outside company do a short-term program, and then we would pick it up and extend it. Now most of the people there were thinking of this as a pilot program, but I wasn't thinking pilot. I had a vision that this would be a 'forever program.'

"Well, they got together after the meeting, and at the next meeting I was the next to last one going in, and the fellow behind me said 'Good morning, Chairman!' So they had done some politicking, and they decided to ask me to chair the group. Now, when they offered the job to me I said, 'Well, this is an honor, but I have a good group now, and I'll probably be around Ford for just three or four more years. If you're real serious about this, I'm going to do it, but I'll need to make some requests."

As it turned out, Red's list of requests had a lot to do with his appreciation for how to get things done in a large, bureaucratic organization. "The first thing I asked for is that they let me take my own minutes. The second request was that we make this an operations project, not an ER (employee relations) project. And the third request was for a high-level steering committee. I had two reasons for asking this. I wanted to ensure senior management involvement, and I wanted to establish an orderly procedure for continuous improvement of the CIRS process. If anyone wants to change something after we get going, they have to get approval from the steering committee first.

"Well, they agreed to all of my requests. My assistant Dick Lebeck takes minutes. A corporate CIRS steering committee was established, consisting of the president of Ford, the controller, the VP of Ford's International Automotive Operations, the VP of Purchasing, the executive VP of Personnel, the VP of Financial Services, and the executive director of Quality, who's my boss. And Jim Emanuel, the former suggestion program coordinator, was assigned to our staff.

"The next thing we had to do was sell it to the rest of the organization. We presented probably 150 times, at various levels in the organization. I continued to gather data from them, continued to redefine the program. From the beginning I had seen it as a long-term program. I tried to get people to imagine what it would be like if five years from now, 15 years from now, every man and woman in the Ford Motor Company would personally understand where we're going, what we'd need to get there, and to have a mechanism through which they could submit their ideas.

"When we finally decided on the initial design of CIRS, we presented it to the steering committee. Their approval was unanimous. That design was kind of like the bible, and I guess I became like the interpreter of the bible. We embellished it, and a lot of people had ideas on how to embellish it, but we had to make sure that it stayed the same person—just gained some weight, maybe—but where it didn't become a totally different 500-pound monster."

I asked Red to talk about the key elements and, in particular, which one he felt was the most vital. "Management commitment is the first—well, maybe it's more like the first three," and he laughed. I challenged him to be more specific, since almost everybody names management commitment as the key ingredient for such an endeavor. Red had an answer waiting. "Here's what **management commitment** means:

- They put it in the business plan.
- They put it in people's objectives.

- They keep score.
- They put good people on the job.
- They allocate resources.
- They insist on participation in training.
- They review performance on a regular basis.
- They recognize people and celebrate achievements.

Red's gloss on the list was this. "One thing I've learned in my 35 years at Ford is that we have a tendency to do things our bosses are going to support. If they never ask about it, we don't do it. We drop it. We watch what they do, not what they say. With suggestion programs, we've been talking about them for a long time, but Ford is now starting to *do* it right, and on a broad basis. We've had pockets before. But now we have a lot of pockets, and they're connected. And we have a plan."

What will it take for CIRS to sustain its success and for all Ford people to be able to contribute in a continuing improvement process? Red's opinion was "You need fully competent, empowered people." Training, Red thought, was important to develop competence, not only in areas involving new technologies, but in the soft skills: how to write, how to speak better, managing conflict, interpersonal skills. "It took a while for Ford to buy into the concept that a guy on the floor needs to be able to manage conflict, but they deal with more conflict than anybody else! "

Red acknowledged that CIRS and what it stood for—an effort to improve upon the way things were being done now—required that people be able to trust one another. In particular, people needed to trust in their bosses when they were asked to participate in an activity that invites at least *implied* criticism of the status quo and those who are seen to maintain it.

"It comes down to the boss being able to say about a problem, 'I want to fix it and I know you do too,' and having people trust him. It takes a long time to build trust," Red acknowledged, "and a short time to lose it." Freedom to fail was a part of this. "The employee that fails is doing you a favor, in that he's helping you to reassess a process. Oftentimes you'll find a flaw in the process, where it's not as good or as robust as it could be."

One of the ongoing discussions within Ford regarding CIRS has been about the use of rewards in the program. Red admitted that he gets pulled into basically the same conversation most of the time. The conversation is typically prompted by someone—almost always a manager—asking why CIRS needs to pay people for their ideas, since they're already getting a salary or an hourly wage.

Red's response is now somewhat practiced. "The problem comes down to this," he begins. "What are we interested in? Are we interested in making sure that none of our employees ever gets a penny more than they deserve? Or are we interested in making sure that this effort is really successful—successful for Ford and for our employees too?" Still, not everybody is convinced by this argument. But Red seems convinced that the rewards element has been critical to CIRS having been as productive as it is. "Rewards are powerful. They make things happen."

When things don't happen, it's often because a management team hasn't bought in yet. "The biggest barrier is still management, but it's coming down now—it's middle management. We've got to get *everybody* in the process. But it's a hard thing. If the plant managers, or the middle managers, don't see what's in it for them, and if it's not in their objectives, then we've got a problem. They have to see some benefit. They need to see the program as part of their objectives, with some measurement so they'll get credit for success. You've got to give them opportunities to take credit for success because they're going to be successful.

"The thing we've got to do, as we try to expand CIRS, is to build on the successes. There are a lot of different pilots, different suggestion programs out there. But we're at the two-year point with CIRS, and it's time to listen to what we've learned. I tell these plant managers, 'I want to listen to you guys. But the rules are these: CIRS is a corporate goal. I will do anything I can to help you enhance the CIRS process. I'll be listening for things to put into the system that will enhance CIRS.'" Reflecting on the challenge of "selling" a corporate goal to the field, Red summed it up this way: "It requires a mixture of understanding, fairness, and firmness."

Red Maynard's assessment of what CIRS has accomplished so far goes beyond the number of participants and the sizeable cost savings generated by accepted ideas. His first comment was this: "We have reaffirmed that we have some very qualified people out there, as good as anywhere in the world. We've created the conditions where they can exercise a team effort and help each other.

"This is a *system* that requires team effort. They're starting to think of the people out there as their customers, and they know they need each other. If we didn't make a nickel on the process, it has still payed off in how we treat each other, and how we treat our customers. When you get people working together on teams, that carries over into everything else."

The other accomplishment Red noted was that CIRS, "by necessity, forces decision-making out there onto the teams. What CIRS is, it's a mechanism for getting out good ideas, but it's also a mechanism through which we can practice becoming better team players. And it affects everything you do. That's powerful, when you think about it. In the past, we've wasted a lot of money training people in team building and not giving them the opportunity to do anything with it. Now they can do something."

Communications

When CIRS is launched at a new division or plant, there is a strong promotional effort made to get everyone involved. A special video describes the purpose of CIRS and candidly reviews the status of employee suggestion activity prior to CIRS. The video also calls attention to Ford's commitment to organizational learning, starting with its founder's development of the first Ford car. "Ford has been learning from its employees since the doors opened," a Ford executive explains. "We want that tradition to continue and, in fact, even do it better."

CIRS takes the *recognition* part of its name seriously. Several communications vehicles are used to keep everyone aware of progress and learning accomplishments. Achievements are reported on the Ford Communication Network, and in an internal publication called *Ford World*. CIRS also publishes its own magazine *Insight* to relate continuous improvement stories and to recognize teams and individual participants.

In addition, department managers and front line supervisors are encouraged to hold recognition "events," and sponsor lunches or other opportunities to recognize CIRS initiatives. The intention behind all these communications efforts is to link companywide CIRS activities through a frequent and consistent message that celebrates success.

Training

All key role players in the implementation of CIRS participate in training. Idea team leaders are helped to develop persuasive arguments and cost benefit analysis when submitting ideas. They are also trained on how to get the maximum level of participation from team members and, generally, how to make their team's efforts successful.

Idea evaluators are prepared to give submitted ideas a fair and expedient reading and to communicate decisions effectively. Training for team leaders and evaluators is typically provided in facilitated group sessions. Other role players in the CIRS process, including supervisors, can receive their training in a variety of ways. While the occasion for the training is the initiation of a CIRS effort, the skills and tactics that are learned enhance ongoing capabilities for knowledge building and organizational learning.

Administration

CIRS will ultimately involve over 300,000 people in Ford facilities around the world. Individuals and teams from these facilities submit ideas which must be recorded and then assigned to an appropriate evaluation group or individual. When decisions are made to approve or turn down an idea, those decisions must be reported and acted upon. Ideas that are accepted prompt awards to originators and assignments to implementers. All the steps after an idea is assigned for evaluation are timed, so as to expedite the process of decision making and implementation. "Timeliness," says Red Maynard, "is the key to success for CIRS."

To make all this happen in an organized and efficient way requires a sophisticated tracking and feedback system. Ford has built an elaborate infrastructure, with its own operations software and dedicated information management staff to move information quickly and accurately. Feedback to originators is critical for continuous learning activity. And not letting any ideas fall through the cracks is critical to the integrity of the process.

Ford's investment in this information system will pay off in several ways. First of all, good ideas will be properly handled. Secondly, small contributions will be able to become bigger improvements through effective dissemination. Finally, individual efforts at knowledge building may be allowed to develop into true organizational learning.

Field Coordination

Every Ford division or plant engaged in implementing CIRS has a local CIRS resource person called a coordinator. The coordinator role is especially important for CIRS to operate well at remote sites, where a headquarters-driven initiative requires some strong local ownership to be successful. Here, the facility coordinator serves as a major information conduit for CIRS. The facility coordinator is also the key contact for CIRS teams, helping them to form, then acting as advocate and coach.

The profile of an effective facility coordinator starts with being close enough to the top to get plant management's ear, yet close as well to the rank and file so as to be credible and trustworthy. Skills include being a good communicator and problem solver, and being willing to take action on behalf of participants or of the process itself. Alton Russell has a reputation of being such a person.

Interview with Alton Russell, Facility Coordinator

Alton Russell is a big man, with a beard. He's the facility coordinator for CIRS at the Nashville Glass Plant, which means he's the pulse of the program there. Alton has worked for Ford for 23 years. He's a second generation Ford employee. He talks about CIRS and his role with an obvious enthusiasm and a sense of hard-won accomplishment

Entering its second year with CIRS, Nashville Glass already has twelve active teams, with about five members to a team. "We launched without much support," Alton remembers. Before CIRS, he had been involved with an earlier suggestion program, which had not been very productive. Few people participated, and ideas that were generated tended to be recognized with "a cookie and a glass of lemonade. "But," he noted, "we still had to bury the old program in order to start CIRS."

Now the two biggest difficulties facing CIRS are getting enough share-of-mind, and overcoming some old mindsets. "Ford is pushing its factories because we're selling a lot of cars. We've got to get floor-level supervisors involved in CIRS, but they can't take any time off. They're averaging 10 to 12 hours a day, seven days a week. And there's no downtime on the machinery to implement ideas. Everybody's busy. It's hard to find the time to get your mind on new ideas. We're constantly pushing schedules. And we can't let our feelings get hurt if our team meeting gets cancelled. "

The old mindsets start with the notion that "Engineers are hired to solve problems and that's what they're paid for." The implication, which runs contrary to the spirit of CIRS, is that only engineers should be concerned about continuous improvement. Then, there are some mindsets about cooperation and working on teams. As Alton observed, "Operators wouldn't talk to maintenance men, and engineers wouldn't talk to either."

Alton Russell and his five hourly coordinators are learning to cope. They've helped teams get organized, and then helped a few get reorganized when it was determined that some team members "were just along for the ride." Nashville Glass employees receive a weekly newsletter that recognizes and congratulates team members who turn in accepted ideas, announces special CIRS "events," and generally promotes CIRS participation.

Alton's latest strategy to get more people involved is described in a recent newsletter.

> Beginning Wednesday, September 7th, the Nashville CIRS Program will begin a 90-day pilot program called the "CIRS SPONSOR PROGRAM." Under this program, ANY CIRS TEAM MEMBER, OR MEMBER OF MANAGEMENT, may "SPONSOR" a NEW CIRS TEAM. . . . As a "SPONSOR," you assist the new team in completing the paperwork and developing the cost-savings of their idea. . . . If the idea is approved and implemented, the "SPONSOR" will be awarded 5% of the total point value for the idea.

Ideas to beget ideas! And Alton claims it's working.

Alton Russell thinks that the greatest CIRS achievement so far at Nashville has been "opening up communications and breaking down some barriers between job classifications. People have swallowed a little self-pride and bought into the process. Our best mix is a team with a cost accountant, an engineer, and people from maintenance and production. They've averaged one to two ideas per week!"

With CIRS entering its second year in Nashville, Alton saw some changes occurring. "We got all the quick fixes out of the way. Now we're seeing bigger ideas, and they're starting to extend the idea evaluation process. We can nickel and dime Ford to death with maintenance ideas, but we *need* to go after the root causes." But in other, equally important ways, CIRS is still the same. "This program is more than the dollars and cents," Alton Russell concludes. "It's people, it's empowerment, it's recognition."

LEARNING FROM SUCCESS

Alton Russell, Red Maynard and their CIRS colleagues get together periodically to check notes, swap stories, and discuss how their continuous improvement process can itself be improved upon. At one such meeting in Dearborn, Michigan, there was concern expressed over changes being proposed and how those changes might cause disruption to the current CIRS process. Conversation went on about some problematic issues, until Red Maynard interceded. "I think," he began, "that the risks [of change] are small compared to the benefits we can get. I'm not asking that we have zero issues to deal with. We haven't done anything that perfectly in this company for a hundred years."

Red Maynard's point is that continuous improvement is not about getting it perfectly, and permanently, right. The real danger to continuous improvement is the delusion that the destination actually gets reached, and the journey stops. When we start worrying about changing something we've grown comfortable with, and rationalize standing pat as the way we'll avoid unnecessary risks, we're working against the open-endedness of continuous improvement and of organizational learning.

Ford is a highly successful company with a successful strategy to keep pushing and stretching ahead. There is no more appropriate place to be about the business of continuous improvement than with your continuous improvement strategy. Red Maynard admitted earlier that he saw his role as manager of this strategic Ford initiative as one of "trying to keep the focus not so much on the details—and there are a lot of details—but on the *purpose* of CIRS." That, we would argue, is the challenge of sustaining organizational learning in a climate of success.

P A R T

III

STARTING FAST AND COMING TO CONCLUSIONS

Companies are successful at organizational learning to the extent that they succeed in overcoming a variety of barriers. The companies we visited in the previous section provide illustrations of how this has been done. For the most part, these examples described ongoing efforts to involve large parts of the organization in continuous learning activity, with *organizational* learning as an outcome.

There is another organizational learning strategy which also addresses several learning barriers that we did not describe. This strategy has been dramatically successful in producing both tangible and intangible results, but it is, by design, of short duration. Its objective is typically to focus a large workforce on work process innovation. Its approach is to energize the people in the organization to make an intensive effort over a short span of time. For many companies, it has represented a way to "get out of the box" (alas, the pun was intended) fast. Chapter 13 examines this strategy and the methods that seem to make it most effective.

In Chapter 14, we try to draw conclusions from the experiences of all the companies we've visited. There are indeed some common patterns to be seen in this experience. And we can infer from them several useful guidelines for making organizational learning happen elsewhere. The chapter closes with a look at the implications these guidelines hold for managers and the role of management in organizational learning.

Chapter Thirteen

A Jump-Start for Learning

The cumulative and self-reinforcing dynamic of learning tends to confer runaway momentum in the competitive race to those who can jump-start learning processes.

Anthony Carnevale[1]

Companies that want to foster organizational learning as a key business strategy may sometimes find it difficult to get participation and buy-in from more than just a handful of employees. And if organizational learning is construed as just a management challenge, then the company is denying itself a valuable *and necessary* contributor to growth and change—the people who do the work of the organization.

How do organizations engage *all* their people in the business of learning and knowledge building? And how can a company energize a workforce that has not been asked in the past to take responsibility for reshaping the ways work is done? Over the past dozen years, we have watched more than 200 companies in a variety of industries adopt a common approach for answering both those questions.

The approach is an intensive, *short-term,* team-based suggestion program, typically focused on cost reduction. It's a way to jump-start the process of organizational learning. But before we begin to profile the experiences these companies have had, we need to establish some background. We'll first have a look at suggestion processes as they've evolved in American business organizations.

SUGGESTION SYSTEMS: A SHORT HISTORY

Suggestion systems have been a part of American business for nearly a century. Eastman Kodak is generally credited with establishing the first suggestion system in the late 1800s, although most systems trace their heritage to the years after World War II. Many of these postwar suggestion systems still exist, relatively unchanged. Traditionally, they've shared the following characteristics:

- Suggestions submitted by individuals.
- Ideas largely undocumented.
- Centralized administration, often by personnel or industrial relations.
- Insignificant awards, made to submitters only, and only for cost savings.

Typically, employees described their ideas on forms and deposited them in a suggestion box. They would be collected periodically, forwarded to an administrator, recorded, and forwarded again to an engineer or a functional manager for a decision. The designated evaluators would often sit on ideas because they were categorically low priority business. The submitter received no feedback on an accepted idea until it was implemented. Somewhat later, the submitter might receive a nominal cash award. The evaluators and those tasked with implementing suggestions received nothing.

Evolving a Better Way

Suggestion systems with these characteristics have, on the whole, produced rather mediocre results. They have suffered from low participation, few submissions, lengthy processing times, and insignificant financial performance. Many have fallen into disuse or have been officially dropped.

More recently, however, the introduction of quality circles and, later, of broader and more systematic quality improvement efforts, has caused suggestion systems to be regarded in a different light. In some cases, companies seeking to install total quality management processes have dramatically redesigned their suggestion systems. The Japanese Kaizen process is often a model for such re-design. In so doing, companies have made suggestion systems an important component of employee involvement and continuous learning initiatives.

Suggestion Systems: Legitimate Expectations

Today, suggestion systems have become a more versatile and so-phisticated device for continuous learning. Operated effectively, they can be expected to contribute to:

- Employee involvement.
- Problem-solving skill development.
- Heightened business awareness.
- Communications across functions and levels.
- Teamwork and team skill development.
- Interdepartmental collaboration.
- "Lowest-level" decision making.
- Significant idea generation and knowledge building.
- Individual and organizational learning.
- Work process improvements.
- Cost savings and revenue enhancements.

SHORT-TERM SUGGESTION SYSTEM DESIGN

All suggestion systems need to be designed according to the kinds of outcomes that are sought. Although the design, or structure, is only one component in a successful suggestion system, it is probably the most definitive one. Suggestion system design generally addresses these issues:

Ten design issues

1. Duration.
2. Participation eligibility.
3. Participation structure: individual, team, etc.
4. Idea eligibility.
5. Documentation requirements.

6. Suggestion process flow.
7. Evaluation process.
8. Financial integrity of approved ideas.
9. Implementation requirements.
10. Reward and recognition.

The short-term, team-based suggestion system, to which we'll now turn our attention, has a basic pattern of design characteristics. To be sure, the company programs that serve as the basis for this chapter's discussion all varied to some extent. But they followed common approaches to the 10 design issues.

Ten design issues: Short-term programs

1. A 12- to 16-week idea generation period, followed by 6 to 9 months of idea implementation.
2. All-employee participation.
3. Team organization, primarily self-formed.
4. Emphasis on cost savings, *without job elimination*.
5. Standard forms for submission and decision communications.
6. Standard process flow, from submission to implementation.
7. Designated evaluation committees.
8. Formal cost benefit calculation.
9. Follow-through on idea implementation.
10. Noncash awards for idea submitters, and other functional roles.

The Value of Teams

In our experience with short-term suggestion systems, team organization leads to higher levels of organizational learning and greater yield in productivity and quality improvement. Teams generally produce more ideas, of greater quality, and of higher value. There are several reasons for team productivity in suggestion systems. We'll call out three of them.

Reason 1: The team format works against inertia. Individuals can *intend* to work up a process improvement idea, but are easily distracted and prone to procrastination. The result is that often the best intentions fail to materialize as action. Teams, on the other hand, have team meetings. If people show up, and the only purpose of the meeting is the business of idea generation, chances are *something* will happen. Teams force action through shared expectations and peer pressure. Teams create their own momentum.

Reason 2: Teams can create more expansive ideas. Team members come with different perspectives and skills. Conversation within the team can build on a small idea and make it bigger. Teams also provide a safe environment for employees to critically examine the status quo, send up trial balloons, experiment, and work collaboratively.

Reason 3: Teams tend to bring projects to closure more frequently. Teams can distribute workload, so tasks can be shared. And because expectations of task completion are created within the team, peer pressure helps to ensure that they are met.

Katzenbach and Smith offer several more advantages to be gained from teams:

> Teams establish communications that support real-time problem solving and initiative. Teams are flexible and responsive to changing events and demands. As a result, teams can adjust their approach to new information and challenges with greater speed, accuracy, and effectiveness than can individuals caught in the web of larger organizational connections.[2]

The Importance of Effective Evaluation and Implementation

Successful suggestion systems ensure that good ideas get implemented. To make sure that ideas reach this final stage, a consistent and expedient evaluation procedure needs to be in place. The programs that were most effective placed evaluation responsibility in a parallel organization of ad hoc management teams. Taking evaluation outside the normal management chain can help get it accomplished more quickly.

When suggesters know their ideas will be evaluated fairly and promptly, they're more likely to submit ideas in the first place. If evaluators are commited to supporting the entire process, from idea generation to implementation (rather than seeing their role as just making approval decisions), the process will work more smoothly and be more productive. And if potential *implementers* are asked to regard idea implementation as an accountability, there's more likelihood of seeing a return on investment.

FIVE SUPPORTING ELEMENTS

Besides a well-designed, dynamic structure, there are five key supporting elements that effective short-term suggestion systems seem to require. They are: communications, workforce preparation, management commitment, operational support, and rewards and recognition.

Communications

Getting maximum participation in a short-term suggestion program requires a bit of promotion and marketing. Participation must be understood as an opportunity—to help grow the company and to reap some personal reward as well. The companies that achieved high levels of participation took special pains to communicate the program as a priority for the organization. A campaign to invite participation was launched, often involving multimedia communications and a lot of direct talk, including all-employee meetings.

Once the program was underway, communications focused on two different objectives. One was feedback: keeping participants regularly informed about the status of their ideas, as well as the status of program accomplishment as a whole. The other objective was to reinforce continued participation through recognition of accomplishments and the celebration of success. Program newsletters were common, as well as a variety of homespun events designed to keep people focused and to have some fun.

Maxwell House kicked off its first short-term suggestion system, called "Maximize Our Future," with a video of several spot interviews concerning people's feelings about the venture. Employees from all parts of the company testified to feeling good about being asked and were eager to show what they knew about how to make things better. One sales representative had this to say:

> Too often with a large company you feel like you're lost in the crowd. If I was given a feeling that I had some responsibility in where my job was heading and what I was able to do within my job, it would trigger more and more ideas, and the more those ideas were responded to, the better I'd feel about my job, and the better I'd feel about my company.

Maxwell House decided to run a second program after the first short term suggestion system had netted significant cost-reduction savings. Again, they launched the program with a video featuring employees. Chuck Phillips, then Maxwell House's president, introduced a team of headquarters and plant employees from Jacksonville who had come up with an ingenious solution to a customer problem in "MAX I." It was a compelling message and helped MAX II produce more learning and more results for the company.

Workforce Preparation

In the programs we've witnessed, teams were given the responsibility to research, document, and value their own ideas. Therefore, team leaders and others involved in the development of ideas received training in the skills necessary to diagnose and solve problems, analyze cost benefits, and present a persuasive case for an innovative idea. Team members also received detailed information on how and where to locate basic pricing information, as well as how to find internal consultants in special knowledge areas like finance and purchasing.

In a broader sense, team members continue their training on accessing and applying information, and on how their company does business, as they build up their ideas. The tasks of research and documentation force team members out into the company for information they don't normally require. The challenge to develop suggestions that will actually bring financial advantage to the company involves for some a different kind of thinking. In particular, it requires that submitters understand how to figure the costs of a present work process and compare present costs to the costs associated with an alternative way, including any one-time start-up costs.

First Maryland Bancorp, with headquarters in Baltimore, ran its team programs to improve productivity in banking operations. More than 3,000 employees participated. About one-seventh of that number received training in team building and cost analysis. A human resources executive, a teller, and an administrative officer made these comments about the learning that occurred.

- People are working smarter. I think it's generated a philosophy within the company of not just doing things because this is the way we've done them but taking a look at them— why are we doing them this way, and is there a better way to do it.

- I didn't really know how much it cost to run a bank. Now I appreciate much more how much things cost, and I learned what other people do. It was good to have a reason to talk to other people around the bank. It's paid off.

- A quantity of workers who never before had been even reasonably cost conscious began to think about the cost of doing business.

Building ownership and competence. Getting prepared to operate an intensive, short-term program involves high levels of commitment and buy-in. Management and union need to plan together. Employees need to be able to raise questions and get good answers.

Solid role preparation is also critical. Senior management must understand system objectives and how to clear the way for smooth sailing. Key role players like team coaches and evaluation committees require special training. Program administrators need to become thoroughly familiar with process flow and with the system's tracking methods. Providing full and intelligible information to all participants and role-specific training for those assuming ad hoc functions were important work preparation tasks in all these programs.

Management Commitment

When Chuck Phillips of Maxwell House appeared as the spokesperson for MAX II's kick-off video, he was demonstrating hands-on ownership in the program. He was also convinced that the suggestion system would serve a significant business purpose. His commitment to the success of the program was based on his understanding of what it could accomplish in the way of organizational learning and productivity improvement.

For Tim Holloway, president of **High Plains Baptist Health Systems** in Amarillo, Texas, management commitment reached even greater heights. At the start of the suggestion program, Holloway pledged to sleep atop the main hospital building if High Plains met its cost-reduction goal. "Take Tim To The Top" was the name given to a display that charted program progress. It showed a drawing of Holloway climbing higher and higher up the side of the hospital as employees moved closer to their goal.

In the end, employees achieved nearly 200 percent of that goal. On a chilly, windy night in October, Tim Holloway kept his promise. He camped overnight on the hospital roof. Other managers at High Plains were prompted to issue their own personal challenges. The head of personnel promised and delivered home-baked cookies for all 1,700 health systems employees. A vice president took the plunge after pledging to skydive for the first time.

While such flamboyance has not been the norm in most of the programs we've seen, management *visibility* in one form or another has been readily apparent. Whether encouraging participation, explaining the importance of the undertaking, or serving as suggestion evaluators or team coaches, managers have been actively engaged in making these programs work. Management commitment means getting visibly involved.

Operational Support

Effective suggestion systems keep track of submitted ideas, from the time of submission to the point of resolution. In the programs we looked at, a sophisticated computer-based tracking process was at the heart of system administration. Program software monitored the status of each idea, "kept time" for those parts of the process (typically evaluation and implementation) that were being clocked, and produced routine status update communications for submitters and other system players.

The possibility of ideas falling through the cracks is one of the real pitfalls for suggestion systems. A related problem is overlong delays in processing suggestions. At **Big Rivers Electric Corporation** in Western Kentucky, a past suggestion system had earned a bad reputation because evaluation of ideas took far too long. "I turned in a suggestion to the old program once," remarked an employee. "It took three years for management to evaluate it, and they finally turned it down."

The new program, called Powerful Ideas, needed an operating system to handle ideas promptly. A system of ad hoc evaluation committees was set up to expedite idea evaluation, with a goal of seven days turnaround. Submitted ideas were tracked carefully, and the more than 1,200 ideas turned in by employee teams during the 12-week program were evaluated within six days on average.

Tulsa Regional Medical Center preceded their suggestion system initiative with an employee satisfaction survey that focused on measuring employees' perceptions of their jobs and work environments. The survey results provided direction for a team program that achieved considerable savings and new revenue. To monitor the status of approved ideas and to ensure the realization of the savings, Tulsa Regional employed a custom-designed computerized audit process. Nine months after idea generation, more than 91 percent of the savings from employee ideas had been implemented.

Rewards and Recognition

At **Pennsylvania Hospital,** founded in Philadelphia in 1751 by Benjamin Franklin, 52 employees won trips to Monte Carlo because their innovative ideas contributed so significantly to the hospital's cost reduction effort. Other employees whose teams submitted approved ideas earned various merchandise awards: exercise equipment, Waterford crystal, computers, and bedroom furniture. The story about employees creating money-saving ideas for their hospital—over $6 million worth—without involving any layoffs was news for *The Philadelphia Inquirer:*

> The top teams vied for the Monte Carlo trip. Not only was a vacation at stake, but so were honor and ego, employees say. . . . Ever gracious, though, many of the winners underscored how the program built

camaraderie throughout the hospital and made them feel more vested in the hospital's future.

"It's not just the awards," said Louis Caliri, materials-management systems manager at the hospital, who had the single largest cost saving idea, at $417,592. "Having an idea that is worthwhile, is accepted and is a benefit to the hospital, that would be enough. But the awards are nice."[3]

The use of noncash awards added elements of excitement and motivation to all these programs, irrespective of industry. Awards were performance based. For teams with approved suggestions, awards were determined according to the approved annualized value of the idea. To further promote active participation, additional awards like a shopping spree in a warehouse full of merchandise or the Monte Carlo trip at Pennsylvania Hospital were announced as program-end bonuses for the most productive teams.

Like team structure, awards seemed to be a force for overcoming inertia. Many of the ideas that were submitted came in early in the programs. One implication here is that the ideas already existed in the minds of the submitters, who only lacked sufficient incentive to bring them forward before. Awards also added an element of promotability to the program. They got the attention of people who might otherwise not have participated. The opportunity to earn something both valuable and desirable seemed like a fair trade-off for the extra effort required and the fact that the organization would profit from that extra effort.

Most programs found ways to honor teams with approved ideas through a variety of recognition strategies, including mention in newsletters and various public ceremonies. Such gatherings were frequently convened by senior management, who looked for opportunities to thank their employees and to encourage continued activity.

But suggestion teams were not the only recipients of rewards and recognition. Practically all of the companies we noted provided award earning opportunities to other program functionaries as well. Team coaches could earn based on the cumulative value of their teams' collective contributions. Evaluators earned if they met preset goals for evaluation turnaround time. And implementers of ideas, an often overlooked group, could earn through complete and timely implementation of approved ideas.

SUSTAINING THE JOURNEY

These intensive, short-term suggestion initiatives created a widely shared feeling of accomplishment. They also raised an awareness of possibilities and an appreciation for the power of employee teams as a force for learning. Opportunities for followup were realized in different ways by the companies that had successfully executed this jump-start activity.

Some chose to repeat the process, allowing a year or more to effectively implement ideas approved from the first round. Others chose to target specific—and often larger and more problematic—improvement areas for special team attention. These areas typically required more deliberate problem-solving effort that also would take more time. Still others used the short-term suggestion system as a way to launch an ongoing TQM, or continuous learning, process.

In most cases, suggestion system activity spurred further skill development by employees. It also led to more flexible organization structures to allow for problem solving across unit and departmental boundaries. The advances to work process and revenue generation brought about by the incremental improvements from suggestion systems and their progeny are considerable. Carnevale makes this point in a discussion of how progressive organizations foster continuous innovation.

> In the traditional economic cycle, innovation is a heroic process easily tracked by economic statistics and patent applications. White-collar and technical elites generate innovations and then design and install specialized machinery and narrowly skilled jobs to exploit them. In the intensified competition characteristic of the new economy, however, inventing and installing major innovations is only the tip of the iceberg of change. Incremental improvement, a process of continuous learning invisible to conventional indexes of economic change, has assumed a growing competitive importance.[4]

Suggestion systems can be a most effective vehicle for stimulating and facilitating innovation in an organization. Short-term systems, properly designed and supported, can help an organization jump-start the process and begin to learn how to make innovation happen.

Chapter Fourteen

Bottom-Up Learning

*In the new economy, learning occurs from the bottom up as well as the
top down.*

Anthony Carnevale[1]

We have seen in the initiatives of American companies from a variety of industries a growing trend toward what we'll call *bottom-
up learning.* Relying upon the entire workforce for innovation and
knowledge building, rather than just on managers and design specialists, these companies are enjoying significant gains in productivity and customer satisfaction. As Carnevale observes,

> The process of continuous learning involves the whole organization,
> not just white-collar and technical personnel. In the new economy,
> learning occurs from the bottom up as well as the top down, often in
> the process of making the good, delivering the service, or interacting
> with the customer. The competitive emphasis on incremental innova-
> tion has turned on its head the traditional heroic view of innovation in
> the economic cycle.[2]

ORGANIZATIONAL LEARNING AS AN
ORGANIZATIONWIDE ENDEAVOR

The purpose of organizational learning is to increase organizational *capability.* Capability, in turn, shows itself in a company's
being able to do the right things right and to do them better and

more quickly than the competition. It also shows itself in a company's being able to reinvent—or redetermine—what the "right things" are in a changing market and to realign accordingly.

Doing the right things right necessarily involves the entire organization. The role of management in tracking market trends, charting a course, deploying resources, and forging alliances is undeniably important. But the role of the rest of the organization in improving performance is also critical to success. Unfortunately, this latter role is often poorly understood and unevenly exploited.

The companies we've described in the previous chapters have found how powerful a force for change their workforce can be. They've invested in strategies that support workforce learning. In turn, they've reaped *organizational* learning dividends. These companies kept a balance between two strategic learning focuses. The first was a focus on the outside environment—the changing financial and technological trends and the changing perspectives of customers and business associates. The second was an internal focus—tapping into the ingenuity and creativity of their employees to reshape and to improve work processes and business operations.

Whenever possible, they integrated these two focuses, so that learning would be more diverse and more expansive. By making the voice of the customer (both internal and external) accessible to increasing numbers of employees, these companies created a basis for more *informed* learning and knowledge building. By enlisting the thinking of suppliers, distributors, and other allies, they made learning a shared business agenda and so reinforced its importance.

The process of learning was, for these companies, not characterized so much by dramatic breakthroughs as by incremental innovation. Innovation was the engine of organizational learning for these companies. Typically, the engine ran at modest speeds, building up steam occasionally, then settled back again. By supporting various team and individual initiatives to *act on* what they knew or were in the process of discovering, these companies were able to leverage their "action learning" potential to maximum advantage.

MAKING LEARNING BEHAVIORS HAPPEN

Organizational learning occurs when organizational behavior reflects openness, experimentation, questioning, risk taking, creativity, and systemic thinking. But how do companies elicit, encourage, and sustain such behavior in their workforce? The cases we've studied are instructive on this question. They seem to suggest that **three strategies** in particular are crucial for facilitating bottom-up learning.

Employee Involvement through Teams

Over and over again we saw that employee teams, either natural work groups or ad hoc teams (or parallel systems), proved successful in overcoming barriers to organizational learning. Teams energized members and gave them confidence to think critically and to challenge the status quo. Cross-functional teams worked against silos and assisted in the crossing of boundaries. And teams took ownership of positive change agendas, focusing on what could be done to solve problems and to improve the current situation.

Information Sharing, Knowledge Dissemination, and Education

Companies that wished to stimulate learning behavior made information—about customers, work processes, and financial practices—more available and accessible to their employees. Much of this information came in the form of performance feedback. Training in problem solving, teamwork, cost analysis, and improving customer satisfaction—to name the most frequently seen topics—was readily provided. And systems to manage and disseminate new knowledge—to ensure that knowledge building had real impact and could be felt broadly across the organization—were created and maintained.

Educating employees about customer expectations, as well as sources of satisfaction and dissatisfaction, helped target learning and make it productive. Educating managers on ways to leverage the knowledge of their employees to create business advances was another productive practice. One interesting consequence was that some managers discovered a viable new role for themselves at a time when many of their past responsibilities were becoming devalued.

Rewards and Recognition

The incentives for engaging in organizational learning come in short- and long-term varieties. Longer term, there is a growing awareness on the part of most corporate employees that career and company successes are dependent on the rate and quantity of learning a company is able to achieve. But it is the short-term incentives, the more immediate rewards and recognition that can come to employees, which have the most impact on learner performance.

Many of the knowledge-building efforts described in this book were deliberately energized by some form of performance-contingent rewards. When knowledge building resulted in measurable gains, employees could often count on sharing in those gains. Companies that actively thanked and congratulated employees for their contributions to organizational learning typically created a deeper and more abiding commitment to learning behavior over time.

LINKING STRATEGIES

A study of recent trends in human resource practices, including the use of nontraditional reward systems, found some interesting correlations among strategies similar to those discussed above. The study was organized by the American Productivity Center and the American Compensation Association. It was called "People, Performance, and Pay."[3]

One of the study's major findings was a rise in the use of employee involvement programs. The four most prevalent kinds of employee involvement, listed below in rank order, were all examples of some form of team activity.[4]

Leading employee involvement practices

1. Small problem-solving groups.
2. Quality circles.

3. Team or group suggestions.
4. Cross-functional employee task forces.

A second major finding concerned the growing frequency of information sharing within major American companies. The study noted two kinds of information sharing in particular:

- Information about the financial and competitive state of the firm.
- Feedback to work groups on the quality and productivity of their performance.[5]

Several of the study's findings acknowledged a widespread increase in the use of nontraditional reward systems, including gain sharing and performance-contingent incentives. Interestingly, this study, as well as two others, identified strong correlations between the incidence of nontraditional reward systems and both employee involvement and information-sharing practices.[6] These three strategies can be seen to reinforce one another and contribute significantly to organizational renewal.

FROM ORGANIZATIONAL LEARNING TO PERFORMANCE IMPROVEMENT

At several points in this book we've alluded to the tendency of learning organization proponents to call out the importance of management learning. More specifically, the literature describes various approaches to helping managers become learners, including the need to challenge and question current understandings. While we don't disagree with this strategy for fostering organizational learning, we haven't found it particularly conducive to action. Nor have we witnessed many instances where this kind of individual learning has readily transferred to organizational learning, as manifested in changes in business performance. We think, in fact, that efforts to promote organizational learning—to become a learning organization—which concentrate mainly on managers are *incomplete*.

From our experiences, we see the primary agenda for managers to be that of sponsoring continuous learning activity as a priority *for all their people.* We see continuous learning comprising habits of inquiry, experimentation, problem solving, and innovation. The action implications for managers in making this happen are both structural and procedural. We see managers needing to learn how to involve people in team knowledge building, to actively share information and provide educational opportunities, and to recognize and reward the behaviors that most frequently contribute to organizational learning. To put this all another way, we see managers fostering organizational learning best by supporting bottom-up learning initiatives.

The companies we've cited saw fit to challenge both managers *and* employees to identify, rationalize, and practice new behaviors. These companies were thus able to use learning to advance their business goals and their organizational competencies. If the notion of a "learning organization" is to have any power and contribute measurably to performance improvement, companies need to embrace a bottom-up approach to learning. That approach, driven by our three key strategies, would seem to have the best potential for action *leading to results.*

NOTES

Preface

1. C. Argyris, "Education for Leading-Learning," *Organizational Dynamics*, Winter 1993, p. 5.
2. D. Garvin, "Building a Learning Organization," *Harvard Business Review*, July–August 1993, pp. 787–79.

Chapter One

1. E. Nevis, A. DiBella, and J. Gould, "Understanding Organizations as Learning Systems," *Sloan Management Review*, Winter 1995, p. 83.
2. Dave Ulrich, Mary Ann Von Glinow, and Todd Jick, "High-Impact Learning: Building and Diffusing Learning Capability," *Organizational Dynamics*, Autumn 1993, p. 60.
3. C. Argyris and D. Schön, *Organizational Learning: A Theory of Action Perspective* (Reading, MA: Addison-Wesley, 1978), p. 20.
4. A. de Geus, "Planning as Learning," *Harvard Business Review*, March–April 1988, p. 70.
5. Argyris and Schön, *Organization Learning*, p. 20.
6. Ibid., p. 28.

Chapter Two

1. D. Schön, *Beyond the Stable State* (New York: W.W. Norton, 1973), p. 60.
2. Argyris and Schön, *Organizational Learning: A Theory of Action Perspective*, pp. 20–24.
3. Ibid., pp. 20–21.
4. Ibid., p. 24.
5. T. Kuhn, *The Structure of Scientific Revolutions* (Chicago: University of Chicago Press, 1962).
6. Argyris and Schön, *Organizational Learning*, p. 26.
7. R. Reich, *The Work of Nations: Preparing Ourselves for the 21st-Century Capitalism* (New York: Alfred A. Knopf, 1991), pp. 174–179.
8. S. Zuboff, *In the Age of the Smart Machine: The Future of Work and Power* (New York: Basic Books, 1988), pp. 73–74.
9. Ibid., p. 74.

10. Ibid., p. 75.

11. M. Knowles, *The Adult Learner: A Neglected Species* (Houston: Gulf Publishing, 1978).

12. R. White, "Motivation Reconsidered: The Concept of Competence," *Psychological Review*, 1959, pp. 297–333.

13. Reich, *The Work of Nations*, pp. 229–233.

14. H. Mintzberg, "The Rise and Fall of Strategic Planning," *Harvard Business Review*, January–February 1994, p. 111.

15. P. Wack, "Scenarios: Uncharted Waters Ahead," *Harvard Business Review*, September–October 1985, p. 84.

Chapter Three

1. P. Senge, *The Fifth Discipline: The Art and Practice of the Learning Organization* (New York: Doubleday), 1990, p. 63.

2. P. Drucker, "Observations of an Influential Bystander," *Insights*, Fall 1991, p. 4.

3. C. Argyris, "Education for Leading-Learning," *Organizational Dynamics*, Winter 1993, p. 9.

4. C. Argyris, *Reasoning, Learning, and Action: Individual and Organizational* (San Francisco: Jossey-Bass), 1982, p. 85.

5. D. Leonard-Barton et al., "How to Integrate Work and Deepen Expertise," *Harvard Business Review*, September–October 1994, p. 119.

6. See G. Hamel and C. K. Prahalad, "Competing for the Future," *Harvard Business Review*, July–August 1994.

7. R. Stacey, *Managing the Unknowable: Strategic Boundaries Between Order and Chaos in Organizations* (San Francisco: Jossey-Bass, 1992), p. 63.

Chapter Four

1. D. Schön, *Beyond the Stable State* (New York: W.W. Norton, 1973), p. 32.

2. C. Argyris, "Teaching Smart People How to Learn," *Harvard Business Review*, May–June 1991, p. 103.

3. C. Argyris, "Good Communication That Blocks Learning," *Harvard Business Review*, July–August 1994, p. 83.

4. E. Schein, "How Can Organizations Learn Faster? The Challenge of Entering the Green Room," *Sloan Management Review*, Winter 1993, p. 88.

5. Jay Hall, *Models for Management: The Structure of Competence* (The Woodlands, Texas: Woodstead Press, 1988), p. 561.

6. Schein, "How Can Organizations Learn Faster?" p. 87.

7. Argyris, "Teaching Smart People to Learn," p. 103.

8. Thomas Davenport, Robert Eccles, and Laurence Prusak, "Information Politics," *Sloan Management Review,* Fall 1992, p. 54.

9. P. Drucker, "Observations of an Influential Bystander," *Insights,* Fall 1991.

10. E. Schein, "How Can Organizations Learn Faster?" p. 86.

11. Srikumar Rao, "The Painful Remaking of Ameritech," *Training,* July 1994, p. 46.

12. Ibid.

13. R. Stacey, *Managing the Unknowable,* p. 47.

14. Argyris and Schön, *Organizational Learning,* pp. 72–73; Schein, "How Can Organizations Learn Faster?" pp. 88–89; and Stacey, *Managing the Unknowable,* pp. 80–81.

15. Argyris and Schön, pp. 72–73.

16. K. Boulding, quoted in Harold Helfrich, *The Environmental Crisis* (New Haven: Yale University Press, 1970), p. 160.

Chapter Five

1. A. Carnevale, "Learning: The Critical Technology," *American Society for Training and Development,* 1992, p. 6; adapted from *America and the New Economy* (San Francisco: Jossey-Bass, 1991).

2. K. George, quoted in "Spotlight: Management Forum," *Health System Review,* March–April 1992.

3. Ibid.

4. B. Osborne, quoted in a postprogram interview conducted by Maritz Performance Improvement Company.

5. D. Mortensen, quoted in a postprogram interview conducted by Maritz Performance Improvement Company.

6. Elizabeth Corcoran, "Learning Companies: Educating Corporations About How People Learn," *Scientific American,* February 1993, p. 107.

Chapter Six

1. M. Kiernan, "The New Strategic Architecture: Learning to Compete in the Twenty-First Century," *Academy of Management Executive,* February 1993, p. 46.

2. P. Wack, "Scenarios: Uncharted Waters Ahead," *Harvard Business Review,* September–October 1985, pp. 73–89; A. de Geus, "Planning as Learning," *Harvard Business Review,* March–April 1988, pp. 70–74; H. Mintzberg, "The Rise and Fall of Strategic Planning," *Harvard Business Review,* January–February 1994, pp. 107–14.

3. P. Senge et al., *The Fifth Discipline Fieldbook: Strategies and Tools for Building a Learning Organization* (New York: Doubleday Currency, 1994).

4. Arlena Sawyers, "Trust in Dealer Top Priority," *Automotive News*, March 28, 1994, p. S–14.

5. Ronald Smothers, "There Are No Accidents, Some Insist," *The New York Times*, May 26, 1993, p. C11.

6. R. Eaton, quoted in the "1993 Report to Shareholders," Chrysler Corporation, p. 8.

7. Ibid.

8. Ibid., p. 7.

Chapter Seven

1. B. Dumaine, "Mr. Learning Organization," *Fortune*, October 17, 1994, p. 155.

2. R. Wratten, "Accountability, Teams, and Rewards: Three Keys to Success," speech delivered at the Fall Conference of the *Quality & Productivity Management Association*, September 13, 1990.

3. L. Csoka, "Closing the Human Performance Gap: A Research Report," (New York: Conference Board, 1994).

Chapter Eight

1. Stanley Slater and John Narver, "Market Oriented Isn't Enough: Build a Learning Organization," *Market Science Institute*, Report Number 94–103, March 1994, p. 11.

2. E. Kidd, quoted in Gail Gilbert, "Rx for Healthcare: CQI and CSI," *The Marketing Research Report* 7, no. 1, 1992, published by Maritz Marketing Research, Inc.

3. Francis Gouillart and Frederick Sturdivant, "Spend a Day in the Life of Your Customers," *Harvard Business Review*, January–February 1994, pp. 122–25.

4. G. Hamel and C. K. Prahalad, "Corporate Imagination and Expeditionary Marketing," *Harvard Business Review*, July–August 1991, p. 83.

Chapter Nine

1. J. Duck, "Managing Change: The Art of Balancing," *Harvard Business Review*, November–December 1993, p. 115.

2. Nirmal Sethia and Mary Ann Von Glinow, "Arriving at Four Cultures by Managing the Reward System," in Kilmann et al., *Gaining Control of the Corporate Culture* (San Francisco: Jossey-Bass, 1986), pp. 408–420.

3. R. Cushman, quoted in "Labor–Management Teamwork Drops $4M to Bottom Line at Armco K.C. Works," *MPIC Journal* (a quarterly publication of Maritz Performance Improvement Company), Fall 1992, p. 5.

4. B. Huselton, quoted on "Profiles of America," January 16, 1994, CNBC-TV.

5. Cushman, "Labor-Management Teamwork," p. 5.

6. E. Schein, "How Can Organizations Learn Faster? The Challenge of Entering the Green Room," *Sloan Management Review,* Winter 1993, p. 91.

7. Jon Katzenbach and Douglas Smith, *The Wisdom of Teams: Creating the High-Performance Organization* (Boston: Harvard Business School Press, 1993), p. 19.

Chapter Ten

1. M. Kiernan, "The New Strategic Architecture: Learning to Compete in the Twenty-First Century," *Academy of Management Executive,* February 1993, p. 50.

2. J. Smith, quoted in "Customer Enthusiasm through Deeds . . . Not Words!" an internal publication of General Motors Corporation, 1994.

3. Kiernan, "New Strategic Architecture," p. 49.

Chapter Eleven

1. D. Schön, *Beyond the Stable State* (New York: W.W. Norton, 1973), p. 30.

2. P. Drucker, quoted in *Wired,* July–August 1993, p. 82.

3. Thomas Ricks, "Warning Shot: How Wars Are Fought Will Change Radically, Pentagon Planner Says," *The Wall Street Journal,* July 15, 1994, p. 1.

Chapter Twelve

1. D. McCann, cited in Robert Bellah et al., *The Good Society* (New York: Alfred A. Knopf, 1991), p. 9.

2. Jay Hall, *Models for Management: The Structure of Competence* (The Woodlands, Texas: Woodstead Press, 1988), p. 560.

Chapter Thirteen

1. A. Carnevale, "Learning: The Critical Technology," *American Society for Training and Development,* 1992, p. 9; adapted from *America and the New Economy* (San Francisco: Jossey-Bass, 1991).

2. J. Katzenbach and J. Smith, *The Wisdom of Teams* (Boston: Harvard Business School Press, 1993), p. 18.

3. Marian Uhlman, "Money-Saving Ideas Bring Rewards for Hospital Staff," *The Philadelphia Inquirer,* June 21, 1994.

4. A. Carnevale, *America and the New Economy* (San Francisco: Jossey-Bass, 1991), p. 79.

Chapter Fourteen

1. A. Carnevale, *America and the New Economy* (San Francisco: Jossey-Bass, 1991), p. 80.

2. Ibid.

3. Carla O'Dell and Jerry McAdams, "People, Performance, and Pay" (Houston: American Productivity Center, 1986).

4. C. O'Dell and J. McAdams, "Major Findings from People, Performance, and Pay," American Productivity Center, 1986, p. 15.

5. Ibid., p. 17.

6. Ibid., pp. 15 and 17. The two other studies are "Capitalizing on Human Assets: The Benchmark Study," 1992, "Organizational Performance and Rewards: 663 Experiences on Making the Link," 1994. Both studies are written by J. McAdams and Elizabeth Hawk and published by the American Compensation Association.

Index

Other books of interest to you from Irwin Professional Publishing . . .

THE POWER OF LEARNING

Fostering Employee Growth

Kris Mellander

Co-published with the American Society for Training and Development

Offers a five-step process that makes learning easier and shows how to get trainees more involved. Shows trainers, managers, and employees how individual learning can contribute to a stronger, more successful organization through different approaches to learning.
1-55623-893-2   225 pages

MANAGING IN THE AGE OF CHANGE

Essential Skills to Manage Today's Diverse Workforce

Roger A. Ritvo, Anne H. Litwin, and Lee Butler

Co-published with the NTL Institute

A blueprint is needed for dealing with complex new issues as they impact hiring, budgeting, rewarding, and other core responsibilities, as the old rules of business are changing fast. Here are insights from 26 top managers—including Ken Blanchard and Trudy Ferguson—on the major issues managers confront today.
0-7863-0303-4   312 pages

FROM VISION TO BEYOND TEAMWORK

10 Ways to Wake Up and Shake Up Your Company

Nicola Phillips

Sums up the most innovative management techniques from around the world—with special emphasis on where the ideas come from and how they are used.
0-7863-0318-2   250 pages

Available at fine bookstores and libraries everywhere.